SpringerBriefs in Global Understanding

Series editor

Benno Werlen, Department of Geography, University of Jena, Jena, Germany

The *Global Understanding* Book Series is published in the context of the 2016 International Year of Global Understanding. The books in the series seek to stimulate thinking about social, environmental, and political issues in global perspective. Each of them provides general information and ideas for the purposes of teaching, and scientific research as well as for raising public awareness. In particular, the books focus on the intersection of these issues with questions about everyday life and sustainability in the light of the post-2015 Development Agenda. Special attention is given to the inter-connections between local outcomes in the context of global pressures and constraints. Each volume provides up-to-date summaries of relevant bodies of knowledge and is written by scholars of the highest international reputation.

More information about this series at http://www.springer.com/series/15387

Jennifer Robinson · Allen J. Scott
Peter J. Taylor

Working, Housing: Urbanizing

The International Year of Global Understanding - IYGU

OPEN

Springer

Jennifer Robinson
Department of Human Geography
University College London
London
UK

Allen J. Scott
Department of Geography and Department
  of Public Policy
University of California
Los Angeles
USA

Peter J. Taylor
Northumbria University
Newcastle upon Tyne
UK

and

Loughborough University
Loughborough
UK

ISSN 2509-7784   ISSN 2509-7792   (electronic)
SpringerBriefs in Global Understanding
ISBN 978-3-319-45179-4   ISBN 978-3-319-45180-0   (eBook)
DOI 10.1007/978-3-319-45180-0

Library of Congress Control Number: 2016949107

Printed on acid-free paper

This Springer imprint is published by Springer Nature
The registered company is Springer International Publishing AG
The registered company address is: Gewerbestrasse 11, 6330 Cham, Switzerland

*The original version of the book
frontmatter was revised: Incorrect preface
text has been rephrased. The erratum
to the book frontmatter is available
at DOI 10.1007/978-3-319-45180-0_6*

Series Preface

We are all experiencing every day that globalization has brought and is bringing far-flung places and people into ever-closer contact. New kinds of supranational communities are emerging at an accelerating pace. At the same time, these trends do not efface the local. Globalization is also associated with a marked reaffirmation of cities and regions as distinctive forums of human action. All human actions remain in one way or the other regionally and locally contextualized.

Global environmental change research has produced unambiguous scientific insights into earth system processes, yet these are only insufficiently translated into effective policies. In order to improve the science-policy cooperation, we need to deepen our knowledge of sociocultural contexts, to improve social and cultural acceptance of scientific knowledge, and to reach culturally differentiated paths to global sustainability on the basis of encompassing bottom-up action.

The acceleration of globalization is bringing about a new world order. This involves both the integration of natural-human ecosystems and the emergence of an integrated global socioeconomic reality. The IYGU acknowledges that societies and cultures determine the ways we live with and shape our natural environment. The International Year of Global Understanding addresses the ways we live in an increasingly globalized world and the transformation of nature from the perspective of global sustainability-the objective the IYGU wishes to achieve for the sake of future generations.

Initiated by the International Geographical Union (IGU), the 2016 IYGU was jointly proclaimed by the three global umbrella organizations of the natural sciences (ICSU), social sciences (ISSC), and the humanities (CIPSH).

The IYGU is an outreach project with an educational and science orientation whose bottom-up logic complements that of existing UN programs (particularly the UN's Post-2015 Development Agenda and Sustainable Development Goals) and international research programs. It aims to strengthen **transdisciplinarity** across the whole field of scientific, political, and everyday activities.

The IYGU focuses on **three interfaces** seeking to build bridges between the local and the global, the social and the natural, and the everyday and scientific dimensions of the twenty-first century challenges. The IYGU initiative aims to raise awareness of the global embeddedness of everyday life; that is, awareness of the inextricable links between local action and global phenomena. The IYGU hopes to stimulate people to take responsibility for their actions when they consider the challenges of global social and climate changes by taking sustainability into account when making decisions.

This Global Understanding Book Series is one of the many ways in which the IYGU seeks to contribute to tackling these twenty-first century challenges. In line with its three **core elements** of research, education, and information, the IYGU aims to **overcome the established divide** between the natural, social, and human sciences. Natural and social scientific knowledge have to be integrated with non-scientific and non-Western forms of knowledge to develop a global competence framework. In this context, effective solutions based on bottom-up decisions and actions need to complement the existing top-down measures.

The publications in this series embody those goals by crossing traditional divides between different academic disciplines, the academic and non-academic world, and between local practices and global effects.

Each publication is structured around a set of key everyday activities. This brief considers issues around the essential activities of Working, Housing and Urbanizing, as fundamental for survival and will complement the other publications in this series.

Jena, Germany   Benno Werlen
May 2016

Contents

List of Figures

List of Tables

List of Boxes

Chapter 1
Introduction

This short book is about cities. Specifically, we are concerned with the overall process of making cities (in other words **urbanizing**) and within this broad theme we focus on the practices of people **working** in cities and their experiences of **housing** in cities. Of course, cities are about much more than jobs and shelter but these two topics provide the basis for understanding how and why people come to cities and live there. Making a living and finding or creating shelter are prerequisites for surviving in the city and they can provide the basis for a fruitful, engaged and satisfying life as a citizen. They also give us some good starting points for thinking about the past, present and future of cities.

The study of cities is particularly important for global understanding. First, and as widely reported in the press, more than half the world's population now lives in urban settlements, and this is an ongoing trend likely to reach the level of three-quarters of the world's population later in the 21st century. Second, the influence of cities extends beyond their specific locations to the point where cities are nowadays increasingly interconnected with one another across the globe. Moreover, almost all humans living on the planet, both urban and rural, contribute to the maintenance and growth of cities through provision of food and raw materials, industrial and service activities, as well as new migrants. These circumstances have led some commentators to suggest that humanity has become an "urban species" and to label our times the "first urban century".

Our century has also been widely termed a "century of crises:" environmental (notably climate change), political (including wars and refugees), economic (especially financial crises and deepening poverty), social (with untenable and rising inequalities), and cultural (including rampant consumerism and growing social divisiveness). Of course, these multiple predicaments are interrelated and all are implicated as both causes and effects in this century's distinctive urban condition. This, then, is a further crucial reason for seeking to understand cities. Moreover, these crises will be faced by urban residents of the future who will need all the ingenuity, collective effort and energy from their experiences to drive humanity in new directions through the 21st century.

© The Author(s) 2016
J. Robinson et al., *Working, Housing: Urbanizing*,
SpringerBriefs in Global Understanding, DOI 10.1007/978-3-319-45180-0_1

There is a fourth and separate reason for studying cities: they are inherently noteworthy as complex aggregations of social problems and social benefits. On the one hand, there has been a long history of observers denigrating cities as dense concentrations of social problems; on the other hand, the broad mass of humanity clearly is strongly attracted to life in cities, which can also be important sites of progressive social change. The excitement of cities—traditionally "streets paved with gold" and today the "bright lights" of the modern metropolis—has also influenced urban scholars and researchers who have become fascinated by the varying capacities of people to make satisfactory lives for themselves within the dense, intricate material and social worlds of cities.

We seek here to capture something of the problems and excitement of cities in terms of four key cross-cutting themes which help us to get to grips with their complexity. These are:

- *The internal spatial structure of cities.* Cities are composed of complex and multifaceted social phenomena. The distinctively urban character of these phenomena emerges out of their forms of spatial organization. For example, do cities enable productive interactions amongst different activities? Is it important to try to keep some activities, such as houses and factories, apart from one another?
- *The diversity of cities across time and space.* One of the important facts about cities is that they vary greatly depending on history and geography. Ancient Mohenjo-daro, Classical Rome, Medieval Byzantium, 19th century Manchester, and 21st century Shanghai can all be described as great cities, but clearly each differs enormously in empirical detail from the others. What can we learn from all these different cities about the challenges and opportunities of urban life?
- *The external relations of cities.* Cities are centres of dense human activities, but they are also connected to the rest of the world. Cities have always had strong external relations, which were crucial in their origins and which, in the era of globalization, have become especially well developed. What is the nature of these wider connections and why do they matter to cities?
- *The internal political conflicts endemic to cities.* The dense concentration of diverse populations and activities in cities means that they are frequently the sites of internal political contestation. Questions of the "right to the city" and citizen demands for equitable outcomes constantly confront urban power structures. Who has the right to shape the future of cities?

We explore these themes in three substantive chapters. The chapter that now immediately follows (Chap. 2) asks how cities came to be, providing a wide survey of the history of *city formation* and focusing on the importance of *the external relations of cities*. These processes take on very different aspects at different times and in different geographical locations so various comparative assessments will also be explored. In Chap. 3 urban economies are described primarily in terms of their function as *centres of work*. The emphasis here is on the many different kinds of economic activities and employment opportunities that are typically found in cities, and how the economic advantages, or *agglomeration economies*, to be gained by firms being located close together sustain the growth of cities. Chapter 4 focuses on *housing* and places special emphasis on the *diversity of cities*. Nonetheless, we identify some common processes and shared issues facing cities across the globe regarding the challenges of providing and accessing shelter, including the different roles of states, markets and residents. In a short concluding chapter we ponder what all this means for urban futures.

In each chapter we present examples from a variety of regions across the world, and there are also text boxes separate from the main text where we offer commentaries on specific topics. A number of relevant figures and tables are provided, and we offer some brief bibliographic information that readers can use to deepen their knowledge of the ideas presented. The book is intended to provide an introduction to urban studies for a wide international audience including students and the general reader.

Chapter 2
Cities in Time and Space

2.1 The Uniqueness of Cities

Cities are distinguished from other human settlements by two key features: they constitute dense and large clusters of people living and working together, and they are the focus of myriad internal and external flows. This is what makes cities uniquely active and vibrant places that are always more cosmopolitan than culturally uniform. Historically these features are expressed in different ways over millennial time as new modes of working and living in cities are generated and diffused. In this chapter these changes are sketched out from the earliest beginnings of urbanization to cities in contemporary globalization.

We begin by exploring when and why cities emerged, and how urbanization today has come to shape life across the entire planet as part of globalization. Looking at the beginnings of the very earliest cities reveals how the genesis of urbanization and the external relations of cities are indelibly intertwined. We will describe how these external relations—links with other cities and with other places —played a crucial role in the creation of the first cities, and also stimulated wider processes of change shaping human history, such as the development of agriculture.

The unique dynamism of cities has enabled them gradually and then rapidly to grow in number and size. Today the flows and networks originating in and circulating through cities are a crucial part of processes of globalization and cities now play a central role in shaping economies and social life worldwide.

2.2 When Did Cities Begin?

An idea which is essential to any understanding of cities is "civilization." We can define this as referring to societies which are spread across relatively large areas of the globe and which have achieved high levels of social and political interdependence.

© The Author(s) 2016
J. Robinson et al., *Working, Housing: Urbanizing*,
SpringerBriefs in Global Understanding, DOI 10.1007/978-3-319-45180-0_2

Cities and civilizations are indelibly linked: cities are nodes which connect many different places together, enabling large-scale interdependence. Additionally, they are the major locales of social change where new forms of working and housing are continually invented and reinvented to create new dynamic and expansive worlds of human activity. Thus cities, through their unique connections, sizes and densities, provide opportunities for people to innovate and adapt their living, always in relationship with many other places.

Initially seven "pristine" (i.e., independently developed) civilizations were recognized in Western scholarship, namely, Mesopotamia (in today's Iraq), Egypt, the Indus Valley (in today's Pakistan), China, Central America and the Central Andes (in today's Peru). Over time, a strongly western-centric perspective in scholarship quite wrongly imagined a trajectory of "civilization" and urbanization stretching over time from Mesopotamia/Egypt through Greece and Rome, culminating in what was seen as the most important civilization, that of modern Europe and America. Perhaps this stemmed from the way in which Europeans at this time saw themselves as uniquely "civilized" compared to other societies. But this intellectual interpretation of the trajectory of cities in time (limited to the last 5000 years) and space (focused on the West) has become increasingly contested as our understanding of early urbanization has progressed through modern scholarship. Instead, we find that many more civilizations existed much earlier in historical time, organized through interconnected cities; and that by far the most significant and long lasting groupings of cities in history were those centred on China.

Initially the identification of early cities and civilizations was based upon excavation of places with large-scale urban monumental remains, notably in Mesopotamia and Egypt. It was the grand urban architectures of the old civilizations that had particularly impressed scholars, but it is becoming increasingly apparent that they had multiple forebears—earlier urban places that developed as regional groups of cities in many different parts of the world. These cities emerged from nodes in successful trading networks where existing traders' camps took on work in secondary production—converting previously traded raw materials (e.g. silicon rock) into manufactured goods (e.g. silicon blades)—and in the tertiary activities this generated (e.g. logistic services such as organization and storage). Where these new arrangements generated increased demand, transitory trading camps grew into concentrations of specifically urban activities that we can identify as the earliest cities.

Although small—the most studied such settlement, Çatalhörük (in modern Turkey) dating from around 9000 years ago, had a population of about 5000[1]— these urban places represented an epochal change in communications, opportunities

---

[1]In this discussion cities are largely represented by their population sizes. This is a pragmatic decision: population estimates represent the only data available to compare cities across multiple regions over several millennia. Of course, all the intricacies of cities—their economic, cultural and social relations—are left out by this approach but nevertheless simple population totals do provide some indication of the logistical issues that arise with large concentrations of people. Every day they have to be fed; fuel for cooking must be obtained; and they need raw materials for working.

and innovation. Compared to previous hunter-gatherer bands of about 150 people, new concentrations of people of this size generated many more social interactions, both within the settlement and through external links. By means of materials processing and trading, such people working in and through interconnected regional groups of small cities created new economic systems.

Such very early cities have been difficult in practice to find. Not only were they without monumental architecture, their buildings, especially ordinary housing, would most probably have been made of materials such as mud and wattle, and these have not survived, especially in wetter regions. Finding urban remains in these circumstances is largely a matter of serendipity: a classic case is Japan's Sannai-Maruyama settlement (Jomon culture) dating back 5500 years with more than a thousand buildings; it was only found during the digging of foundations for a new baseball stadium (see Box 2.1). However, archaeologists using new airborne laser scanning technology are finding new networks of ancient cities in places such as Amazonia and Cambodia as well as uncovering extensions of known networks in places such as Egypt.

Box 2.1 Making early cities

Cities were not invented as a complete urban package. The small city that features most in the debates on early urbanization, Çatalhörük (in Anatolia, Turkey, some 9000 years ago), illustrates this well: it had no streets! In this settlement, houses abutted each other and ladders were essential to movement between houses within the city. Ladders enabled entrance to houses through holes in their roofs for people travelling across the urban space created by the combined roofs. The invention of streets to replace ladders as more convenient means of urban movement was to come later.

That there was no simple blueprint for inventing cities is shown in African indigenous urbanization in the Middle Niger region (West Africa possibly more than 3000 years ago). Here the layout was the opposite of Çatalhörük; it was an urban complex with large open expanses up to 200 m wide between a central cluster of buildings and surrounding smaller clusters. Its similarity to Çatalhörük is in its concentrating people in new original formats thereby enhancing inter-personal communication and opportunities for innovation.

Initially, the Middle Niger settlement complexes were not considered to be "urban" not only because of their unusual structure but also because the indigenous people were assumed not to be capable of something as sophisticated as city-building. Such sentiments were to be found with other early city sites: Great Zimbabwe and associated settlements in southern Africa (c. AD 1300), early Mayan cities (in Central America c. 300 BC), and Cahokia (Mississippian

---

(Footnote 1 continued)

These inputs will be complemented by diverse outputs including waste and products for export. Size of population, then, can be taken as a rough indicator of flows in and out of a city.

culture c. AD 1100) were all examples of urbanization denied because local non-European peoples were not considered feasible city-makers by Europeans although all are now studied as candidates for early urban process.

Today, searches for early signs of urbanization are among the most exciting research developments in urban studies. In particular, evidence is mounting, including from remote sensing, that the dense tropical forests Europeans encountered in their exploration of the world may not be pristine nature as originally and continually thought. In particular, the Amazon forest may have housed a large urban civilization, including a city "fourteen miles long" on the banks of the Amazon river, and similar claims are being made for the forests of Congo and South East Asia.

2.3   The Emergence of Large Cities

The multiple beginnings of early cities in regional groups around the world included what we today would consider to be quite small cities with population estimates of only a few thousand; much larger cities are found later in traditionally recognized civilizations (see Box 2.2). And size does matter: the larger the city, the more social interactions and therefore the greater the chances for generating innovations. Thus, although Mesopotamia's cities are no longer seen as being the first cities, they do constitute the first network that incorporates large cities. For instance, about 5000 years ago Uruk in Sumer (lower Mesopotamia) had a population estimated at 80,000. This counts as a truly new world of working and housing; think again of the logistics involved. Just the daily feeding and disposing of the waste of this number of people was a massive undertaking. It is when cities reach this size that evidence about their form and functions (including their innovations) becomes increasingly available. In Uruk's case these include the crucial twin inventions of accounting and writing; the new profession of scribes is an archetypal urban occupation group.

Box 2.2 Making the first large cities

Early cities relied upon creating a hinterland where the development of agriculture satisfied the increased demand for food. But these first cities proved not to be resilient: their rudimentary agriculture put heavy demands on the soil. To keep up with a growing urban population, agricultural production gradually moved further and further from the city. At some point transport of food to the city became too difficult to maintain. Thus early cities appear to last several generations but are then abandoned leaving their erstwhile hinterland as waste land, sometimes referred to as an 'empty quarter' reflecting its desolation.

To create large cities required a new way of providing food: sustainable agriculture to enable resilient cities. The solution was irrigation agriculture based upon controlling flooding that continually replenished the soil. Thus the first large cities are associated with the great traditional civilizations are on the lower reaches of major river systems—the Tigris-Euphrates in Mesopotamia (Iraq), the Nile in Egypt, the Indus in Pakistan and the Yellow (Hang Ho) and Yangtze rivers in China. Of course these river systems also facilitated trade—water transport was much more efficient than land transport before modern industrialization. Hence there was a coming together of two requirements for a massive new phase or urbanization: trade generating economic spurts and sustainable productive agriculture.

Subsequently these civilizations became dominated by new imperial political structures wherein the largest cities were capital cities, politically favoured by tribute rather than economically favoured by trade. Economic generation of the largest cities only returned with the onset of modernity after 1500.

Although Uruk is the largest city in early Mesopotamia it should be seen as part of a Sumerian network of cities, specifically eleven cities with a total population of over a quarter of a million. It is such great extensions of urbanization that created what were considered the initial civilizations. Similar spurts of large city growth occurred in Egypt, China and India perhaps slightly later, and later still in the Americas and sub-Saharan Africa. In this way cities became an established part of human history exhibiting continuity to the present. Two urban trajectories were of special importance, namely, a "West" trajectory combining Mesopotamia and Egypt (and covering western Asia, Mediterranean/Europe), and an "East" trajectory centred on China (also including Korea and Japan). Between them these two regions constituted the nine biggest city networks before 1800 (i.e. prior to modern industrialization). Each of these networks had ten or more cities with populations over 80,000 within a two hundred-year period (Table 2.1). Here we find a very clear challenge to the traditional West-centric narrative concerning the history of urbanization, for it is the dominance of Chinese networks of cities that stands out. Note that five (the majority) of these very large city networks are found in the East compared to the West. More importantly, the East trajectory shows a growth in size and numbers of cities over time in a single, broad regional grouping whereas there was no such coherence in the historical urbanizations of the West. Put simply, it is only in East Asia that we find an historical development encompassing a strong and continuous urban pattern.

Why, then, is there such a strong traditional emphasis on the role of the West in the study of large-scale historical urbanization? We would argue that this is the result of the modern West as the dominant region of the modern era bringing its own forebears to the front in writing world histories. Correcting this basic geographical misunderstanding is crucial for two reasons. Historically, we would

Table 2.1 The largest historical city networks[a]

Large city networks	Number of large cities	Total population contained in large cities[b]
East Asian networks:		
Sino-centric: 400–300 BC	14	2,430,000
Sino-centric: AD 700–800	12	2,584,000
Sino-centric: AD 1300–1400	14	2,593,000
Sino-centric: AD 1500–1600	15	2,935,000
Sino-centric: AD 1700–1800	21	5,648,000
Networks in the "West":		
Roman: 200–100 BC	10	2,025,000
Roman: AD 200–300	15	5,963,000
Islamic: AD 900–1000	16	9,320,000
Early modern: AD 1500–1600	13	1,722,000
Worldwide network:		
AD 1900	357	106,446,000

[a]Large cities are defined as cities with populations of 80,000 and above; civilizations including 10 or more of such cities within a period of two centuries are identified
[b]Note that these numbers do not represent the total urbanized population in these world regions because the many more cities with populations below 80,000 are not included

expect the Chinese as inhabitants of the region of great cities to be the most innovative (see Box 2.3). From a contemporary standpoint, global understanding of China's long urban tradition is necessary for placing China's great current urban revival in a broader perspective.

Box 2.3 Innovations from the cities of China before 1800

As the centre of the world region with a continuous trajectory of city networks over millennia, it is to be expected that China should be the locale for urban innovations *par excellence*. And this is indeed the case. Joseph Needham, the great scholar of China in the mid-20th century, catalogued 262 "inventions and discoveries" and some of the more important that were converted into practical innovations are listed below:

Abacus; Acupuncture; Anemometer; Axial rudder; Ball bearings; Belt drive; Blast furnace; Callipers; Cartographic grids; Cast iron; Chain drive; Chess; Crossbow; Decimal place; Dominoes; Drawloom; Firecrackers; Flamethrower; Folding chairs; Gear wheels; Gunpowder; Harness; Hodometer; Hygrometer; Iron-chain suspension bridge; Kite; Lacquer; Magnetic compass; Mouth organs; Multiple spindle frame; Oil lamps; Paper; Planispheres; Playing cards; Porcelain; Pound-lock canal gates; Printing; Relief maps; Rotary fan; Spindle wheel; Steel production; Stirrup; Stringed instruments; Toothbrush; Trip hammers; Weather vane; Wheelbarrow; Winnowing machine; Zoetrope.

This is a very impressive list and raises the question as to why China was not the region to create a global urbanization. In fact China never came close to such an outcome, remaining a traditional empire until incorporated into the western economic sphere in the 19th century. As a traditional empire, tribute from a large and productive peasantry was the main source of wealth for a political elite so that, despite the large sizes of traditional Chinese cities they remained demographically a minority.

But focusing on these two major urban developmental trajectories neglects other parts of the world that did not have so many large cities but nevertheless did create some very large urban centres of their own. Historical demographers identify 63 very large cities (i.e. cities with over 150,000 inhabitants) before 1800. Of these, 17 reached the impressive size of half a million inhabitants—they are large cities even by present day standards. All these cities are mapped and named in Fig. 2.1 where the continuity of cities, their resilience, is also shown in their durability over time—cities marked by the darkest circles are those which have been more consistently present over time. Again, it should be remembered that the cities that are mapped represent only the largest cities in the urban groupings with many more cities below the size threshold, including many important but smaller urban settlements in regions not included in the map (notably in the Americas). Many of the cities named on Fig. 2.1 are well-known (e.g. Constantinople, today's Istanbul) but there is a large number that do not have wide recognition today. For instance, about five hundred years ago, Vijayanagara[2] in today's India was larger than Constantinople and was probably the second largest city in the world at that time. Therefore the key point of the map is to show the sheer extent of large-scale urbanization before modern industrialization.

But let us now draw your attention to the bottom section of Table 2.1. The story told through large city populations now veers in a new direction. There is a profound transformation in the urban process in terms of both urban scale and geography after 1800 that signals a broader societal change. This is the modernity invented in the West based upon capitalism where economic factors dominate to the benefit of cities. Thus the growth of very large cities in Europe and the Americas in the 19th century is not the outcome of a long historical "Western" trajectory of urbanization as traditionally argued; rather it represents a disruption, a new modern trajectory that leads to contemporary globalization.

By the end of the 19th century all networks of cities were incorporated into a single world system. In this new modern world the number of large cities and their total populations are at a completely different level compared to previous large city networks. And it is the West (now including the USA) that is conspicuously the terrain of the new large cities. This change represents the key urban growth phase of the process that has culminated in the 21st century's status as the first "urban

---

[2]Near contemporary Hampi in Karnataka State, South India. Today it is a world heritage "site.

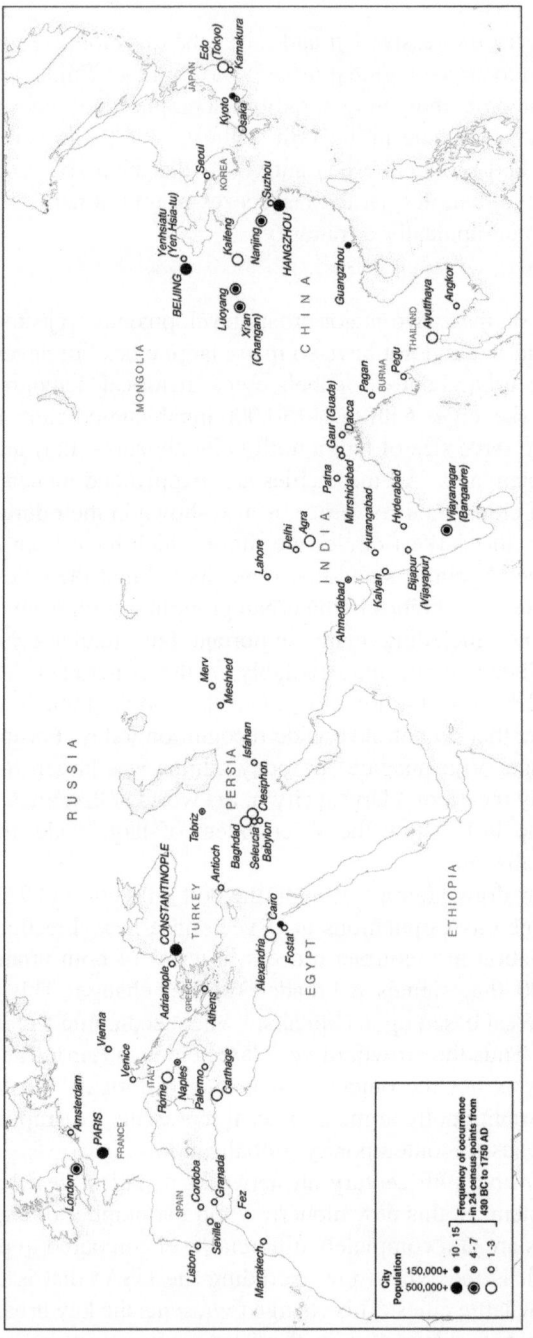

Fig. 2.1 Cities with populations estimated over 150,000 before 1800

century." What caused this shift? The answer lies in the significant changes that took place in the relationships between cities and their wider environments, especially the political structures of states and empires.

Before the modern era, the world's population was overwhelmingly rural; even in the most urbanized regions, city populations largely remained below 10 % of the total. In this rural world, the largest cities were the capital cities of world empires. The dominant activities in these cities revolved around political control and administration together with servicing the needs of the political elites. Tribute brought from across the empire supported large urban populations. In these traditional empires there was also an urban hierarchy consisting of inter-related cities, provincial political centres and economic centres of trade and production.

In China, self-ascribed as the "Middle Kingdom", the capital city at the centre of urban networks changed with the dynasties but the rest of the urban system was stable over time. In the West, the great capital cities of early Empires, i.e. Rome and Baghdad, persisted over time and were huge centres of consumption, but they were far apart in time and space. Neither of these cities was to be part of the early modern city network of the West, which gradually emerged after 1500 (Table 2.1). In fact, the most dynamic areas of this early modern network were in northwest Europe, centred on Amsterdam, so it was towards the edge of the traditional urban networks of the "civilized" world of the West that this important new urban network emerged (see Fig. 2.1). As a new trajectory, it had a much smaller overall population relative to the other established historical networks (Table 2.1), making it appear to be an unlikely starting point for the unprecedented growth that the West experienced under industrial modernity after 1800.

To understand this radical shift in the scale and geography of modern urbanization from the long pre-modern history, we once again find ourselves thinking about how the course of history has been profoundly shaped by the dynamic nature of cities, especially their capacity to stimulate innovations and foster external relations.

2.4   Urban Take off: Modern Cities in Globalizations

The solution to the puzzle as to why the most important modern urban developments emerged in one of the previously lesser urbanized areas of the globe, is to be found in the political context of early modern cities rather than in their demography. Not being part of an overarching empire meant generally that there was no need for large political centres, which explains the initially smaller size of the cities in the early modern Europe (Table 2.1). But this also meant that the relative autonomy of these cities was enhanced. Without an overarching traditional empire, political authority was divided into multiple territorial states. And, crucially, this fragmentation of political power changed the relations between political and economic elites. In traditional empires political elites had dominated the commercial classes; in the new modern cities, this situation changed into a much more balanced relation between political and economic forces. New relations between cities and states came into being, giving more autonomy to cities, and leading to the intensification of their dynamic role as centres of innovation. With cities as innovation hubs under reduced political restraint, the outcome has been a speeding up of social change, the hallmark of modernity. Thus, the regional clusters of centres of economic innovation that have changed our world developed in urban conditions which were relatively independent of political power. Innovation in these centers has been above all reflexively related to their underlying economic dynamics. The following are the three main regional clusters of modern economic innovations.

First, the Dutch cities were the great early modern centres of commercial innovation in the 17th century and operated in a loose political structure, the "United Provinces," that was arguably not a fully formed state, or if so, was a "merchant's state" where the political elite exercised only limited power.

Second, in the late 18th and early 19th centuries, the great wave of innovations underlying what we call the Industrial Revolution originated in the towns and cities of northern Britain, far removed from the political centre of London.

Third, the rise of the USA as an economic power in the late 19th century came as a consequence of innovations in the cities of the Manufacturing Belt stretching from New England to the Midwest, within a weak federal state when Washington, DC was still a small city of minor significance.

These three urban powerhouses of modernity each relied on extensive external connections, growing through plunder and trade (including the Atlantic trade in slaves) and through colonial (territorial) and commercial (market) expansions. Their dynamism accelerated economic development in new uneven geographies then emerging and leading to the globalized world familiar to us today. As the first of these economic powerhouses, Dutch cities had a key *regional* effect on urbanization, leading the shift of urban economic growth from Mediterranean Europe to north Atlantic Europe. This had subsequent global ramifications but was not itself fully global. However, the other two powerhouses, focused on cities in the UK and the USA, were the sites of immense urban growth (as indicated by the data for 1900 in Table 2.1). In this new world-making process of urbanization we can identify three related but distinctive phases of *globalization*, as a result of worldwide economic inter-connections.

2.4.1 Imperial Globalization

This first globalization came to its fruition some time around 1900, though its influence was still being strongly felt over the first half of the 20th century. The founder of modern geopolitics Sir Halford Mackinder referred to it as "global closure." Imperial globalization derived from the political process whereby the world was carved up into competing sea empires of European states (and latterly involving the USA and Japan). Economically this process operated worldwide—forming the original or "old international division of labour"—where colonies, ex-colonies (Latin America), and countries subject to unequal treaties (economic opening via political pressure, notably in China) supplied food and raw materials for European markets. This stimulated the emergence of three types of fast-growing cities: (a) the new imperial capitals in Europe, the largest being London and Paris; (b) industrial cities in Europe, the largest being Manchester and the Rhine-Ruhr urban region; and (c) dependent cities beyond Europe dealing with the logistics of relaying products to Europe and coordinating emerging regional economies, the largest being Buenos Aires, Shanghai and Calcutta (Kolkata). A parallel regional structure also developed in North America where New York functioned as the business and commercial capital complemented by industrial cities in the Manufacturing Belt (such as Chicago, Cleveland and Pittsburgh) and local supply cities in the West (Denver, San Francisco), and the South (Atlanta, Dallas).

2.4.2 American Globalization

This form of globalization grew in the first half of the 20th century out of the regional arrangements just described above. New York became the world's leading financial centre. At the same time, a burgeoning mass production system in North America and Europe was complemented by the development of mass consumption. Increased productivity translated into higher wages so that levels of consumption soared in what J.K. Galbraith in the 1950s famously referred to as the "affluent society." Across US cities, suburbia became the primary landscape of this new world of consumption, epitomized by the case of Los Angeles. Americanization is the term used to describe the diffusion of this way of living beyond the USA. It encompassed Western Europe over the "long post-war boom" after 1950, and then spread to middle classes across the world including the former Second World of communist countries later in the century. The shopping mall came to symbolize modern cities in the American mode across the world. In addition, an important political change affected much of the world: the post-1945 era was also a time when many former colonies became independent countries. In seeking to promote their own national development paths these countries created new political economies increasingly centred on their capital cities. Hence, most countries in what came to be called the "Third World" in the Cold War political climate of the time developed "primate city" urbanization with one city becoming very much larger than the rest. The corresponding nationalist agendas in these countries, while fostering new manufacturing concentrations and civic investment, ironically neglected urban development beyond the capital. Instead, territorial policies in hinterland areas displayed a strong commitment to rural development, especially in Africa and Asia. The extreme case of this kind of policy is represented by China, where urbanization actually declined in the 1960s.

2.4.3 Corporate Globalization

The current situation is one that can best be described in terms of corporate globalization. This represents a progression of Americanization but is increasingly shaped by other centres of economic influence, notably in Asia. The main agents of the previous globalization were US multinational firms with highly developed export capabilities. Then, through the 1970s, the newly emerging communications and computer industries started to herald a new world of near instantaneous flows of information worldwide. Corporations were thus increasingly able to operate as complex global entities, a shift that greatly facilitated the relocation of industrial production to cities in poorer countries so as to take advantage of cheap labour. This development was complemented by states pursuing neoliberal, free-market oriented policies thus opening up national economies to global economic competition and enabling corporations to invest widely in different countries. These corporations came to be characterized as *trans*national, and then, more simply, *global* corporations. US firms represent the main instances of these economic goliaths but they are now joined by firms from many other countries, including China. In the latter case a rigorous export growth policy initially based upon cheap labour resulted in the largest rural-urban migration flow in history, more than 100 million people between 1990 and 2005. The majority of China's population is now urban. The outcome of these overall trends has been a highly integrated world economy undergirding what urban sociologist Manuel Castells has termed a global network society. Castells identifies global cities and a broader world city network as a spatial organization challenging traditional international relations of states in the 21st century.

From Mackinder's political global closure to today's world of transnational corporations, these three globalizations represent a sequence of overlapping processes with the earlier phases not disappearing but fading into the later, so that all are present in contemporary corporate globalization.

2.5 Global Urbanization Inside Out

Historically, urbanization has been closely associated with economic growth, and cities have typically been the main motors of this growth. The usual result is that the richest countries characteristically had the largest cities But this is not always the case today (Table 2.2; see also Box 2.4). This reversal is clearly shown in Table 2.3. In the development of imperial globalization in the half-century up to 1900 the fastest growing cities were European and US industrial cities and capital cities, plus a few key ports located in the rest of the world. In the development of American globalization in the next half-century this general pattern continued but with a clear tendency for US cities to eclipse their European counterparts. However with the advent of corporate globalization in the second half of the 20th century this

Table 2.2 Today's largest cities (termed Megacities)

2016 Rank	City	Country	Population[a]		
			2016	1900	1800
1	Guangzhou	China	47,700,000	585,000	800,000
2	Tokyo	Japan	39,500,000	1,497,000	685,000
3	Shanghai	China	30,900,000	619,000	90,000
4	Jakarta	Indonesia	28,100,000	115,000	53,000
5	Delhi	India	26,400,000	207,000	140,000
6	Seoul	Korea (South)	24,400,000	195,000	194,000
7	Karachi	Pakistan	24,300,000	114,000	[b]
8	Manila	Philippines	23,300,000	190,000	77,000
9	Mumbai	India	23,200,000	780,000	140,000
10	Mexico City	Mexico	22,100,000	368,000	128,000
11	New York	USA	22,000,000	4,242,000	63,000
12	São Paulo	Brazil	21,800,000	239,000	[b]
13	Beijing	China	21,100,000	1,100,000	1,100,000
14	Osaka	Japan	17,800,000	970,000	383,000
15	Dhaka	Bangladesh	17,600,000	90,000	106,000
15	Los Angeles	USA	17,600,000	107,000	[b]
17	Lagos	Nigeria	17,100,000	38,000	[b]
18	Bangkok	Thailand	16,900,000	267,000	45,000
18	Moscow	Russia	16,900,000	1,120,000	248,000
20	Cairo	Egypt	16,800,000	595,000	186,000
21	Kolkata	India	16,000,000	1,085,000	162,000
22	Buenos Aires	Argentina	15,800,000	806,000	34,000
23	London	Great Britain	14,400,000	6.480,000	861,000
24	Istanbul	Turkey	14,300,000	900,000	570,000
25	Tehran	Iran	13,700,000	150,000	30,000
26	Johannesburg	South Africa	13,400,000	173,000	[b]
27	Rio de Janeiro	Brazil	12,700,000	744,000	29,000
28	Tientsin	China	11,400,000	700,000	130,000
29	Paris	France	11,200,000	3,330,000	547,000
30	Kinshasa	Congo (Dem. Rep.)	10,600,000	[b]	[b]
31	Bangalore	India	10,500,000	161,000	50,000
32	Nagoya	Japan	10,400,000	260,000	92,000
33	Lahore	Pakistan	10,200,000	200,000	30,500
34	Chennai	India	10,000,000	505,000	110,000
35	Xiamen	China	10,000,000	100,000	65,000

[a]Note that estimates of megacity populations vary widely because of the difficulty of defining how far large city regions extend, often involving combining cities in multi-nodal urban complexes. Here we use "major agglomerations" from www.citypopulation.de
[b]Population below the bottom threshold of the data (20,000 in 1800; 30,000 in 1900)

pattern has been completely reversed. The fastest growing cities in this period are not found in the regions of economic dominance. Rather, of the 25 cities in this period listed in Table 2.3, seven are from South Asia, five from Latin America, four from the Middle East, and three each from East Asia and Sub-Saharan Africa. Only three of these cities are located in the USA, and two of these, Miami and Dallas, are ranked at the bottom of the list in 23rd and 25th places, respectively.

Box 2.4 Megacities

The United Nations Human Settlements Programme (UN-Habitat) is concerned with urban problems—shelter, waste disposal, traffic, air pollution, water supply—emanating from growth of very large cities. This organization uses the term "megacity" to describe the largest cities in the world; originally focusing on cities with populations above 8 million, now the threshold is 10 million. Table 2.2 shows the 35 cities that qualify in 2016. The population estimates are for "urban agglomerations," broadly densely integrated city regions, rather than "metropolitan areas" based upon administrative units. The former are favoured because they represent the actual urban geography of the cities rather than their political designation. The table shows cities of amazing sizes: five over 25 million with Guangzhou approaching 50 million. For most of these cities the rise to "mega" status has been relatively recent (Table 2.3). Thus, compared with the eight cities from the richer countries of the world economy (Europe, USA, Japan), the other 27 cities are critically struggling to cope with the challenges of their recent rapid expansion in size with far fewer material resources. China is a special case: the five cities featured in the table are the tip of an iceberg reflecting the largest rural-urban migration ever recorded. Although residents of these poorer megacities face many problems, we should not underemphasize the opportunities that are also offered. These huge agglomerations of people are a maelstrom of ideas, inventions and innovations for survival, adaptation, advancement, cooperation and much else in all realms of human activity, not least in creating jobs and shelter. Whether these social interactions are largely organized through formal or informal arrangements, legal or illegal in relation to government regulations, it is in megacities and other very large cities that people will be forging an urban future in the 21st century.

The current situation, then, is one characterized preeminently by a world-wide network of major urban centres. Some have been termed, "megacities," by reason of their large populations typically in the multiple millions (see Box 2.4). More generally, "world cities" (also called "global cities") can be identified by their functions in integrating the world economy—their deep insertion into global capitalism and their significant role in shaping global economic and social processes. Although many of the most prominent of these cities are located in the

Table 2.3 Fastest growing cities, 1850–1900, 1900–1950 and 1950–2000[a]

1850–1900	1900–1950	1950–2000
Chicago	Los Angeles	Lagos
Buenos Aires	Houston	Dacca
Leipzig	Dallas	Khartoum
Pittsburgh	Hong Kong	Kinshasa
New York	Detroit	Phoenix
Berlin	Sao Paulo	Surat
Newcastle	Shanghai	Fortaleza
Dresden	Seoul	Chittagong
Boston	Seattle	Belo Horizonte
Budapest	Buenos Aires	Delhi
Hamburg	Atlanta	Karachi
Rio de Janeiro	Toronto	Shantou
Warsaw	Tokyo	Seoul
Munich	Washington	Taipei
Birmingham	Moscow	Bogota
Prague	San Francisco	Ankara
Vienna	Santiago	Medellin
Tianjin	Nagoya	Lahore
Manchester	Singapore	Rawalpindi
Copenhagen	Montreal	Kabul
Shanghai	Rome	Izmir
Philadelphia	Osaka	Tehran
Barcelona	Sydney	Miami
Osaka	New York	Monterrey
Baltimore	Milan	Dallas

[a]The top 25 cities are listed for each period in order of their population growth

economically dominant economies of the Global North, increasingly cities in East and South Asia and elsewhere are playing a significant role in globalization processes. We should also recognize that a plethora of smaller urban centres beyond the mega- and global/world cities exist across the entire globe; these also play an important role in global economic and social processes and some of them are marked by exceptionally rapid recent growth.

The following two chapters now explore how it is that cities both shape and are shaped by the array of broad processes we have discussed so far, focusing on two of the most significant elements of life in cities, namely, making a living and finding shelter. It is only after basic needs in regard to work and home are satisfied that citizens can fully partake in wider aspects of city life. In the end, this form of life lies at the core of the future of the planet, socially, economically, politically, and culturally, for it is in cities that the most advanced and innovative trends of social change are concentrated.

Further Reading

Abu-Lughod, J L (1989) *Before European Hegemony: The World System, A.D. 1250-1350.* Oxford: Oxford University Press
Arrighi, G (2010) *The Long Twentieth Century: Money, Power and the Origins of our Times.* London: Verso
Cronon, W (1991) *Nature's Metropolis: Chicago and the Great West.* New York: Norton
Jacobs, J (1969) *The Economy of Cities.* New York: Vintage
Jacobs, J (1984) *Cities and the Wealth of Nations.* New York: Vintage
Taylor, P J (2013) *Extraordinary Cities: Millennia of Moral Syndromes, World-Systems and City/State Relations.* Cheltenham, UK: Edward Elgar

Additional Data Sources

For city populations worldwide from 1998 to the present: Major agglomerations - www.citypopulation.de
For worldwide commercial connections between cities from 2000 to the present: Globalization and world cities – www.lboro.ac.uk/gawc
For global historical demographic data on cities there are two sources: 1. Chandler, T (1987) *Four Thousand Years of Urban Growth: An Historical Census.* Lewiston, NY: Edwin Mellen Press (provides city populations from 2250BC to 1975). 2. Modelski, G. (2003) *World Cities, -3000 to 2000.* Washington DC: Faros 2000.
The United Nations is the major source for worldwide data and although most of its publications describe states (i.e. UN members) there are now key sources for urban studies: 1. UN-Habitat - unhabitat.org. 2. World Urbanization Prospects - http://esa.un.org/unpd/wup

Chapter 3
Working

As we saw in the previous chapter, the history of urbanization all around the world is long and multifaceted. Thus far we have considered this history without paying much attention to the internal dynamics of cities. In this chapter, we set out to describe some of the production and employment features of cities. These features are not only of critical importance in their own right, but also shape urban patterns and urban growth trends as a whole. In turn, cities constitute major foundations of the growth and prosperity of modern economies. The discussion that follows focuses mainly, but not exclusively, on cities in the modern era.

3.1 Working and Living in the Urban Milieu

In their internal organization, cities appear at first glance to be composed of a bewildering and incomprehensible mass of heterogeneous objects and activities. More careful scrutiny, however, reveals that there are some fairly systematic organizing principles that can help to moderate this complexity and to bring it into more understandable order. In particular, one way of clarifying at least some of the puzzling diversity that characterizes the internal organization of the city is to describe it in terms of three broad structural features comprising (a) production space (areas where goods and services are created), (b) residential space (the parts of the city where workers live and carry on much of their social life), and (c) circulation space (where movement through the city occurs, and notably the daily movement of workers between production space and residential space). The interweaving of these three spaces delineates the spatial layout (spread) and internal interactions (flows) of every city, though their specific shape and form vary widely across the cities of the world. Frequently, these spaces interpenetrate and overlap with one another in various ways, as, for example, when residential space is also used for production.

© The Author(s) 2016
J. Robinson et al., *Working, Housing: Urbanizing*,
SpringerBriefs in Global Understanding, DOI 10.1007/978-3-319-45180-0_3

Of course, the city as a whole is always considerably more substantial than this simple threefold schema suggests, and we would need to introduce many more social, cultural, and political attributes in order to get a more complete sense of the urban in its full complexity and vitality. But this schema is useful for our discussion both here and in the next chapter because it points to some of the most basic structural elements of the city. Thus, production space is where employment sites are concentrated and where people earn a living; residential space is where urban dwellers live, socialize, pursue family life, and raise children; and circulation space provides channels of access between different urban activities, most especially between home and work. One of the most obvious features of the modern city is the daily cycle of urban life in which large numbers of individuals—perhaps the majority of the adult urban population—leave their residences in the morning and journey through the city in order to reach their places of employment or livelihood; and then in the late afternoon and early evening proceed through a reverse set of motions as they travel from work back to home. This picture is modified in cities where many people live and seek livelihoods in the same parts of the city, whether because work is informal or home-based or because accommodation is provided in factory complexes. It is also worth bearing in mind that "home" involves considerable domestic labour, usually disproportionately borne by women.

In any case, without work, whether formal or informal, and the productive activities that support it, urbanization as we know it could not survive. Indeed, one of the primary reasons for the existence of cities in the first place is their function as centres of economic life. By the same token, production and work activities are the principal drivers of urban development, and the basic factors that induce the growth (and decline) of cities.

3.2   From Craft Production to Capitalist Industrialization

Even before the historical transition to industrial capitalism in the 17th and 18th centuries, the large city populations recorded in the previous chapter were engaged in distinctive forms of urban life revolving around production and work, and above all traditional small-scale craft activities focussed on outputs like textiles, ceramics, furniture, and leather goods, whether for internal consumption or for trade. Some of this trade involved exchange for agricultural products originating in surrounding agricultural communities; some of it, usually the greater part, involved exports to more distant locations in exchange for imports.

With the advent of capitalism and the rise of factory-based types of production, new modes and patterns of urbanization began to make their historical and geographical appearance. The most advanced expression of this new order of things is represented by Britain after the early 18th century when the Industrial Revolution started its inexorable rise. As in earlier phases, external connections were crucial in the development of cities; in particular, Britain's industrialization was intimately associated with the import of commodities (i.e. industrial inputs such as cotton and foodstuffs such as wheat) from various colonies and settler communities around the world.

The factories and workshops that proliferated as early industrialization processes in Britain ran their course were located above all in areas close to energy sources such as waterpower and coalfields. However, as the steam engine came to supplant the water mill, coal rapidly became by far the dominant source of energy, especially in the major manufacturing sectors of the 19th century such as textiles, metal goods, and machinery. Clusters of factories and workshops comprised the functional nuclei of the rising manufacturing towns. Immediately around them, extensive tracts of working-class housing also came into being as people (often displaced agricultural labourers from the surrounding countryside) moved into the towns in search of employment.

For much of the period of classic industrialization, workers in the main British manufacturing towns formed a downtrodden and impoverished proletariat, vividly described by Engels in his book *The Condition of the Working Class in England*, which portrays the horrors of working-class housing conditions in Manchester in the middle of the 19th century. At this time, capitalist forms of industrialization and urbanization were also developing rapidly in different parts of Continental Europe and the United States, with resulting urban social problems much like those of Britain. Early and at first very tentative forms of town planning, such as street cleaning, public health measures, and housing legislation, were introduced in attempts to mitigate some of these problems. Also, as the 19th century wore on, the sporadic passage of relatively progressive social legislation (including the official authorization of trade unions) gradually, and in noticeably diverse ways in different countries, brought about improving wages and living standards for the working classes.

The accelerated economic growth and the associated expansion of towns and cities in Western Europe and North America over the 19th century meant that these areas steadily consolidated their already significant position as a dominating core of the emerging world system, though in practice, the core itself was divided into very unequally developed regions (in particular, some were focused on agriculture while others experienced industrial development and accelerated urbanization).

In relation to this core, the rest of the world could be described as a periphery spread out over Africa, Asia, and Latin America, much of it subject to colonization and economic dependency in various ways. As a corollary, the organization of world trade in the 19th century and well into the 20th century adhered to the logic of an international division of labour in which the periphery produced raw materials (especially agricultural products and minerals) to supply the factories and feed the workers of the core countries while a portion of the manufactured products of the core was exported to the periphery (usually at very unfavorable terms of trade). The net consequence was greatly enhanced growth in the core and a steadily widening gap between the wages and living standards of industrial-urban workers in the core and the mass of workers in the periphery. In relation to this system, urbanization under the aegis of colonial capitalism in the periphery was dominated by the expansion and development of *entrepôt* (i.e. warehousing and exporting) cities at coastal sites like Accra, Calcutta (Kolkata), and Lima, which also hosted emergent production and servicing functions. Urbanization also proceeded at resource exploitation locations, trading posts, and administrative centres at more inland locations. Intertwined with the expanding colonial system of urbanization were networks of earlier indigenous cities and settlements. In these ways the first or imperial globalization was constituted as a system of uneven and hierarchical relationships between different places across the world.

3.3 The Mass-Production Metropolis and Beyond

By the beginning of the 20th century, industrialization in the core capitalist countries was moving into a new and dynamic phase marked by the rise of mass production and its deployment in process industries like steel and chemicals and assembly industries such as cars and machinery. In the context of the new rounds of economic growth set in motion by these events, urbanization in the core capitalist countries expanded at a notably rapid pace. The most dramatic expression of this turn of events was the emergence of the so-called Manufacturing Belt of North America, stretching from the Midwest of the United States to New England plus adjacent parts of Canada (Fig. 3.1). An echo of this development also occurred in

Fig. 3.1 American Manufacturing Belt. *Source* A. Pred, The concentration of high value-added manufacturing. *Economic Geography*, 1965, 41: 108–132

the guise of a smaller and more fragmented Western European counterpart extending discontinuously from the Central Valley of Scotland and the Midlands of England, through northeastern France, much of Belgium and southern Holland to the Ruhr region of Germany. Both of these macro-regions constituted the economic engines of North America and Western Europe over the first half of the 20th century and well into the 1960s. As such, they constituted by far the most important centres of industrial production and working-class life in the more economically developed parts of the world.

Among the principal metropolitan areas in the North American Manufacturing Belt were Chicago, Detroit, Cleveland, Toronto, Montreal, Pittsburgh, and Boston. Representative cities of the equivalent Western European Belt were Birmingham, Lille, Roubaix, Essen, and Dortmund. The urban areas of these two great industrial macro-regions came to be marked over much of the 20th century by distinctive social and occupational structures reflecting the division of labour in metropolitan manufacturing systems. On the one side, white-collar workers formed an elite group of managers, professionals, and technical employees who oversaw production and commercial affairs. On the other side, large cohorts of blue-collar workers made up the manual labour force in the primary mass-production plants and their associated input suppliers. The main industrial cities of North America and Western Europe also attracted significant inflows of migrants. Thus, over the middle decades of the 20th century, African-Americans moved northwards from Southern states like Alabama, Georgia, and Mississippi into the American Manufacturing Belt in search of work; and Eastern and Southern Europeans also migrated in large numbers into major industrial centres not only in Europe but also in North America.

In the 1950s and after, manufacturing activities also started to grow rapidly in a number of cities in selected parts of the world periphery (e.g. Brazil, Chile, Nigeria, India, Malaysia, South Korea, and Indonesia). Much of this growth was based on local import-substitution policies involving the expansion of industrial capacity designed to displace mass-produced goods imported from the core countries. Various cities in Asia, (e.g. Kuala Lumpur and Taipei), Africa, (e.g. Lagos and Accra) and Latin America, (e.g. São Paulo and Mexico City) that were affected by this trend also acquired significant working class populations whose numbers were boosted significantly by rural-urban migrants. In some of these places, industrial workers along with mine-workers and other urban dwellers played an important role in anti-colonial politics.

The mass-production system revolved centrally around the assembly-line in large dominant plants constituting the functional core of the system. The suppliers of these plants formed tiers of direct and indirect input producers. The system was also associated with many different kinds of administrative, commercial and financial functions. Some of these functions were located inside the factories in the main manufacturing cities themselves, but large numbers were also accommodated in specialized office districts in primate cities like New York, London, Paris, and Berlin, or in regional centres such as Johannesburg, Hong Kong and Buenos Aires. In addition, activities like the stock market and merchant banking were concentrated in the same cities, as they had been since the time of imperial globalization when they played a strong role in the coordination of financial and commodity flows through international networks. These primate cities were accordingly centres where the more prosperous business and professional classes congregated, and this state of affairs was in part reflected in the superior cultural infrastructures and services that these places had to offer. Even so, certain inner-city areas of these primate centers were typically occupied by small-scale labour-intensive workshops producing outputs like clothing, furniture, jewellery, printing services, while significant tracts of their more suburban fringes were colonized by large factories.

Over the first half of the 20th century, despite interludes of financial crisis and war, this industrial-urban system consistently engendered rising wages and high levels of prosperity in the core countries. In particular, after the Second World War, the so-called "Long Post-War Boom" lasting until the late 1960s, created unprecedented levels of economic well-being for workers in North America and Western Europe, and helped to underpin the *Pax Americana* under which the post-War international political settlement was partly stabilized. These developments coincide with the period that we earlier described as "American globalization".

By the 1950s, many parts of the world periphery (now coming to be known as the "Third World") were assertively gaining their independence from the former colonial powers, and were seeking their own pathways to growth and development. As we have seen, some of the larger Third World countries also attempted at this time to promote indigenous industrialization programs on the basis of import substitution. Many cities in these countries experienced waves of in-migration from surrounding agricultural areas where standards of living were significantly lower and where technical and organizational changes in agriculture were also leading to population displacement. Hence population growth in these cities was at times far in excess of actual labour demands giving rise to shanty towns with large numbers of economically and politically marginalized individuals making a living on the basis of informal work (i.e. work that is officially unrecorded and/or evades regulation and taxation, or is illegal). The urban areas most affected by this syndrome, (i.e. mega-cities such as São Paulo, Lagos, Mumbai, and Manila) often came to be described as being "macrocephalic," signifying their relatively overgrown dimensions in relation to other cities in the same country, and even by comparison with large cities in richer countries.

3.4   Crisis and Renewal

3.4.1   Industrial-Urban Restructuring

By the late 1960s and early 1970s, the Long Post-War Boom in the core capitalist countries was beginning to show signs of exhaustion. The causes of this change are too complex for a full treatment here, but one of the important contributory factors was certainly a rapidly accelerating tendency for manufacturing activity to disperse away from traditional industrial cities and regions and to seek out alternative locations where land and especially labour were relatively cheap. This process took the form of the relocation of branch plants, first of all to the southern states of the US (the "Sunbelt") and less developed regions of Europe (like the Italian *Mezzogiorno*) and then to various parts of the periphery of the global economy. The resultant decline of productive activity in the previously dominant industrial cities of North America and Western Europe provoked deepening fiscal crises and rising unemployment, so much so that by the mid-1970s, the American Manufacturing Belt itself was coming to be known as the "Rust Belt," a term that captures the extensive dereliction, abandonment, and job loss that came to characterize the region at this time. Detroit, the former world capital of car production, was notably devastated by decentralization of production capacity and employment. Even today much of Detroit remains in a state of advanced decay and its current population is just half of what it was at the beginning of the 1970s (see Fig. 3.2).

Other major urban casualties of this phase of global urbanization were in some of the poorest countries in the world, which were especially badly affected by the economic crises in the US and Europe in the 1970s. Encouraged to take on initially cheap loans (available as a result of an expanding supply of petro-dollars) to cover the costs of import-substitution policies and declining income from exports of primary commodities, the burden of these loans increased greatly as interest rates rose during the crisis. Cities in countries which had seen significant modernization, such as Zambia or Kenya, saw a collapse in investment, infrastructure provision and

Fig. 3.2 Empty Packard plant and surrounding derelict land, Detroit, 2010. *Source* A.J. Scott and E. Wyly, Emerging cities of the third wave. *City: Analysis of Urban Trends, Culture, Theory, Policy, Action*, 2011, 15: 289–321

even basic services. City life and work became more precarious and informalized—at times even accompanied by reversal of migration as well as by remittances of food and income from the countryside to the city.

From the early 1970s onwards, the outflow of branch plants and investment capital from the core countries of capitalism to selected sites in the world periphery continued apace. Favored destinations for this relocation activity were export processing zones in Hong Kong, Singapore, South Korea, Taiwan, Mexico and Brazil, and subsequently in emerging Chinese industrial cities, such as Shenzhen and Shanghai. In tandem with these developments the old international division of labour involving the flow of raw materials to the core and the reverse movement of manufactured products to the periphery started to give way to a new dispensation in which unskilled blue-collar manufacturing jobs were increasingly being relocated to the cities of the periphery while the more skilled white-collar functions of management, R&D, and commercialization remained concentrated in the large metropolitan areas of the core countries. Accordingly, it seemed for a while as though the long-term economic geography of capitalism was destined to coincide with the establishment of a durable division of global space into two specialized zones, one devoted more or less exclusively to white-collar employment and the other to blue-collar employment. It turned out, however, over the 1980s and 1990s, that much of the world (and especially the urban world of work) was due to develop in some surprisingly unforeseen ways.

3.4.2   The New Capitalism and Urban Occupational Change

The foundations of the mass-production system and its satellite production activities coincided preeminently with capital-intensive electro-mechanical technologies. But after the late 1970s and early 1980s, a new technological regime based on digitized methods of calculation, information storage, and communication started to emerge and began insistently to penetrate into all sectors of the capitalist economy, including not only manufacturing, but also, business, financial, and other service sectors. As it happens, the 1980s also coincided with the collapse and reorganization of the old tripartite international order designated in terms of First, Second, and Third Worlds. This shift was manifest in the rise of corporate globalization as the concrete expression of a steadily integrating worldwide capitalism reinforced by a turn to pro-market neoliberalism in the policy sphere.

The new capitalism that started its historical ascent at this time was distinguishable not only by a rapidly evolving technological environment, but also by the displacement of the mass production system as the leading edge of growth and innovation. Expanding new and revitalized sectors like high-technology and software production, business and financial activities, personal services (ranging from medicine to tourism), and a vast array of cultural and creative industries including film, music, architectural design, and media rose to prominence as significant foci of capitalist development. Of special interest here is the fact that these sectors are

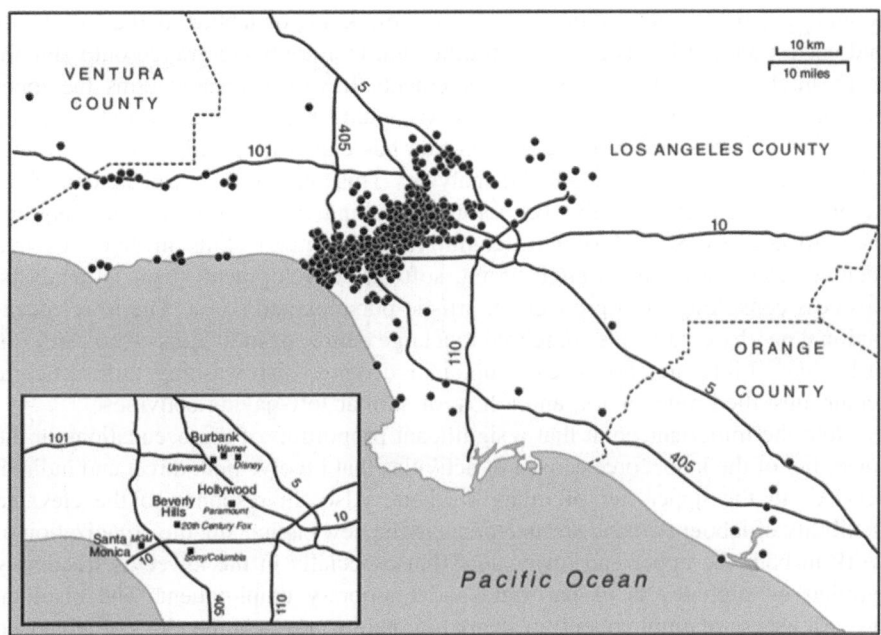

Fig. 3.3 Locations of motion-picture production companies in Los Angeles. Many different kinds of industries at different periods of capitalist urbanization evince this same tendency to form specialized industrial districts in the city. Clustering of individual production units is induced in large degree by their transactional interrelationships and by their joint dependence on a common labour market. *Source* A.J. Scott, A new map of Hollywood: the production and distribution of American motion pictures, *Regional Studies*, 36, 2002, 957–975

also overwhelmingly located in large metropolitan areas, not only in the traditional core countries of world capitalism, but now, too, in many big cities in former Third World countries. Firms in these sectors are strongly susceptible to agglomeration economies in the sense that as they cluster together so the costs of interfirm interaction and labour recruitment tend to fall while innovation is stimulated by the co-presence of many different producers and associated interfirm flows of information. Hence firms in these sectors frequently locate in close proximity to one another in the city to form specialized industrial districts, including high-technology clusters, office districts, and quarters devoted to creative and cultural production (see, for example, Fig. 3.3). These sectors and the work arrangements peculiar to them now account for some of the most dramatic and far-reaching shifts in patterns of urbanization today, especially but not exclusively in the more advanced capitalist countries.

As digital technologies and corresponding organizational readjustments penetrate into the more advanced sectors of contemporary capitalism, the economic and social character of the cities where these transformations are most in evidence is shifting rapidly. This is apparent not only in new and revitalized clusters of economic activity within cities but also in new kinds of labour market structures and corresponding forms of social stratification that are being grafted onto and are increasingly replacing older social arrangements. In very schematic terms, the upper occupational tier characteristic of the new capitalism in large cities today can be identified in terms of what Richard Florida has called a "creative class" or what others have referred to as "symbolic analysts." This upper tier is made up chiefly by highly qualified and usually well-remunerated individuals whose work requires them to exercise well developed cognitive and cultural skills in activities that include scientific research, engineering, software development, financial analysis, business consulting, film production, artistic pursuits, and so on. The lower occupational tier, by contrast, is composed to a large degree of individuals who carry out tasks like child care, house cleaning, taxi driving, dish-washing, infrastructure repair, unskilled office work, and a host of similar low-paying activities.

Note the important point that a significant proportion of the occupations in the lower tier of the labor force consist of activities that involve both direct and indirect services to the upper tier of urban workers. Also, in response to the elevated flexibility of labour demand arrangements in the new capitalism, the organization of work in both the upper and lower tiers (but especially in the lower) is frequently typified by high levels of part-time and temporary employment. The resultant precariousness of employment for many low-paid workers in the cities of advanced countries, and the stark contrasts between skilled, well-paid work, and unskilled poorly paid work resembles in some respects the more strongly informalized and unequal labour markets of cities in middle and lower income countries.

An exemplary case of how work in many large cities is changing in response to these developments can be found in the shifting occupational structure of the Los Angeles metropolitan area over the last decade or so. Thus, between 2000 and 2012, the number of blue-collar workers in manufacturing in Los Angeles declined by as much as 31.8 %. Over the same period, the number of workers in high-level or cognitive-cultural occupations grew by 39.0 % while workers in low-wage service occupations increased by 18.6 %. A large proportion of the latter workers is comprised of ethnic and racial minorities and immigrants from low-wage countries. A further symptom of the changing structure of rewards and penalties in urban life today is the great expansion in the number of homeless individuals in large cities. It is estimated, for example, that some 30,000 homeless individuals are now living in and around the downtown area of Los Angeles.

Urban economies across many cities in Africa and Asia, too, are marked by high levels of "informality," involving small-scale production, repair and recycling, marketing of agricultural goods, and retail trade. In India, for example, estimates placed informal employment at 83 % of non-agricultural employment in 2000, and in Kenya at 72 %. Across much of Africa informal employment stands at over 80 % of the working-age population in cities. Some of this informal activity is caught up in long distance trading networks, as for example in the case of consumer goods transported from Southeastern China to West Africa. Global corporate producers, too, are frequently connected to the informal economy as in the case of production activities that are linked to poorly regulated factories and sweatshops. In addition, formal workers in many cities rely on informal supplies of housing and services.

3.5   Urbanization and Work in the 21st Century

In the 19th and much of the 20th centuries we could speak reasonably meaningfully about a world system comprising a core and periphery each with distinctive patterns of economic development and urbanization. Echoes of this core-periphery termi-nology continue to resonate in what scholars in the 21st century often refer to as the Global North and the Global South, indicating respectively the wealthier and poorer areas of the globe, and the often stark inequalities existing across different parts of the world. As globalization proceeds, however, the mutual interpenetration of the North and the South becomes increasingly pronounced. Unskilled immigrants from the Global South converge persistently and in substantial numbers on the cities of the Global North where they for the most part find jobs entailing low-wage menial activities. Conversely, direct foreign investment in "emerging economies" remains high despite a slowdown of economic growth in these countries in recent years. At the same time, while the most advanced sectors of capitalism today are concentrated in the cities of the North, many are also firmly implanted in the cities of the South, which by the same token are also playing an increasingly important role in exporting high-technology, business service, cultural, and allied products to the North.

Systematic evidence of this changing economic geography can be found by scrutinizing Table 3.1, which lists 75 cities identified by MasterCard as the most attractive worldwide centres for advanced business and commercial activity in 2008. This particular ranking has its deficiencies, but it is probably about as good a representation of a first-cut urban-economic geography of the more prosperous side of the new capitalism as we are likely to get at the present time. Not surprisingly, Table 3.1 reveals that the cities of the Global North are clearly dominant, with London, New York, and Tokyo occupying first, second, and third places, respec-tively. However, a number of cities from the former Third World also rank highly, notably Singapore, Hong Kong, Seoul, Taipei, and Shanghai, all of them in Asia. In addition, as we scan further through the rankings a large number of cities from other parts of the erstwhile Third World also increasingly make an appearance, and cities like these will undoubtedly improve their rankings in the future.

In spite of the eclipse of the mass production system and the rise of new configurations of business and advanced industrial activity, traditional manufac-turing has by no means disappeared and is still quite evident in many cities around

Table 3.1 The top 75 Worldwide Centers of Commerce as defined by Mastercard Worldwide

Rank	City	Country	Index value	Rank	City	Country	Index value
1	London	United Kingdom	79.17	39	Dusseldorf	Germany	50.42
2	New York	United States	72.77	40	Geneva	Switzerland	50.13
3	Tokyo	Japan	66.60	41	Melbourne	Australia	49.93
4	**Singapore**	Singapore	66.16	42	**Bangkok**	Thailand	48.23
5	Chicago	United States	65.24	43	Edinburgh	United Kingdom	47.79
6	**Hong Kong**	Hong Kong	63.94	44	**Dubai**	United Arab Emirates	47.23
7	Paris	France	63.87	45	Tel Aviv	Israel	46.50
8	Frankfurt	Germany	62.34	46	Lisbon	Portugal	46.46
9	Seoul	South Korea	61.83	47	Rome	Italy	45.99
10	Amsterdam	Netherlands	60.06	48	**Mumbai**	India	45.71
11	Madrid	Spain	58.34	49	Prague	Czech Republic	45.50
12	Sydney	Australia	58.33	50	**Kuala Lumpur**	Malaysia	45.28
13	Toronto	Canada	58.16	51	Moscow	Russia	44.99
14	Copenhagen	Denmark	57.99	52	Budapest	Hungary	44.52
15	Zurich	Switzerland	56.86	53	**Santiago**	Chile	44.49
16	Stockholm	Sweden	56.67	54	**Mexico City**	Mexico	43.33
17	Los Angeles	United States	55.73	55	Athens	Greece	43.25
18	Philadelphia	United States	55.55	56	**São Paulo**	Brazil	42.70
19	Osaka	Japan	54.94	57	**Beijing**	China	42.52
20	Milan	Italy	54.73	58	**Johannesburg**	South Africa	42.04
21	Boston	United States	54.10	59	Warsaw	Poland	41.26
22	**Taipei**	Taiwan	53.32	60	**Shenzhen**	China	40.04
23	Berlin	Germany	53.22	61	**New Delhi**	India	39.22
24	**Shanghai**	China	52.89	62	**Bogotà**	Colombia	38.27
25	Atlanta	United States	52.86	63	**Buenos Aires**	Argentina	37.76
26	Vienna	Austria	52.52	64	**Istanbul**	Turkey	36.14
27	Munich	Germany	52.52	65	**Rio de Janeiro**	Brazil	35.91
28	San Francisco	United States	52.39	66	**Bangalore**	India	35.78
29	Miami	United States	52.33	67	St. Petersburg	Russia	35.55
30	Brussels	Belgium	52.16	68	**Jakarta**	Indonesia	35.40
31	Dublin	Ireland	51.77	69	**Riyadh**	Saudi Arabia	35.37
32	Montreal	Canada	51.60	70	**Cairo**	Egypt	35.29
33	Hamburg	Germany	51.53	71	**Manila**	Philippines	35.15
34	Houston	United States	51.30	72	**Chengdu**	China	33.84

(continued)

Table 3.1 (continued)

Rank	City	Country	Index value	Rank	City	Country	Index value
35	Dallas	United States	51.25	73	**Chongqing**	China	33.13
36	Washington DC	United States	51.19	74	**Beirut**	Lebanon	31.81
37	Vancouver	Canada	51.10	75	**Caracas**	Venezuela	26.11
38	Barcelona	Spain	50.90				

Names of cities lying in peripheral and formerly peripheral areas of the world system are set bold

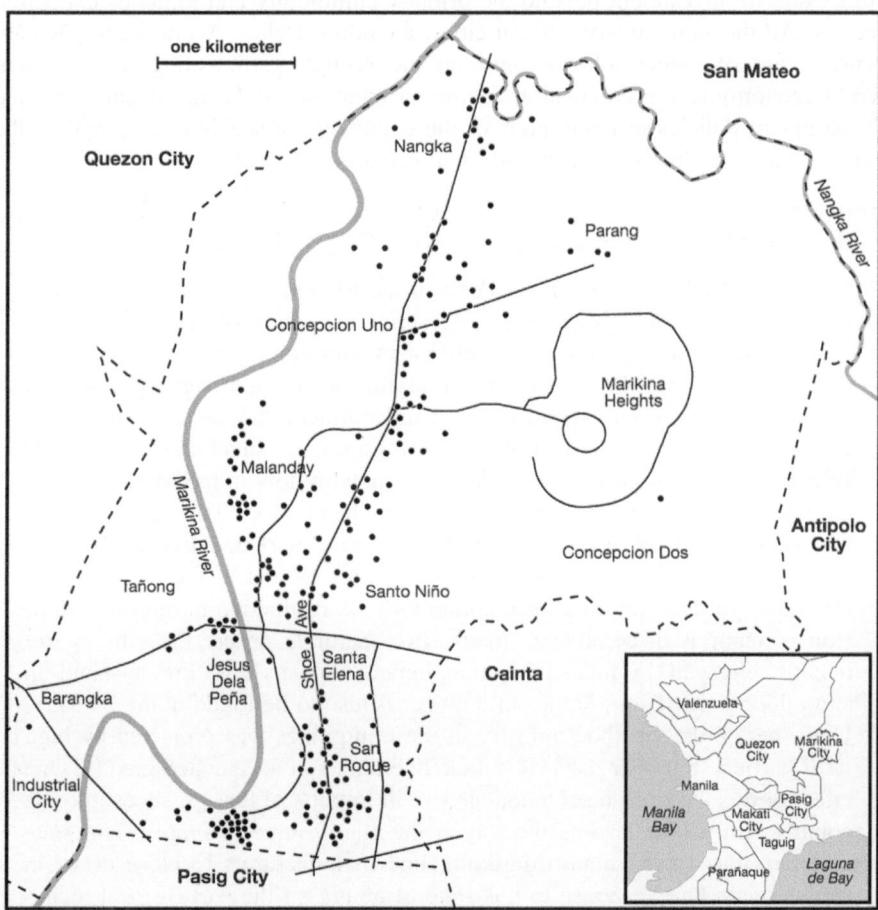

Fig. 3.4 Geographic distribution of shoe manufacturers in Marikina City, Philippines. Each dot represents one manufacturer. *Barangays*, or local administrative divisions, within Marikina City are named, as are adjacent municipalities. The inset shows the location of Marikina City within the Manila Metropolitan Area. *Source* A.J. Scott, "The Shoe Industry of Marikina City, Philippines: A Developing Country Cluster in Crisis", *Kasarinlan: Philippine Journal of Third World Studies*, 20, 2005, 76–99

the world cities, and nowhere more so than in Asian cities where foreign and domestic owned factories abound. China exemplifies this point dramatically. Additionally, industry in the form of small-scale, labour-intensive production can be found extensively in poorer countries, as exemplified by the information provided in Fig. 3.4 and Box 3.1 where the shoe industry of Marikina City in the Philippines is described. At the same time, marginalized informal and precarious labor continues to proliferate in large cities in poorer countries (Fig. 3.5). The recent expansion in manufacturing and other economic activity in more dynamic Asian and other cities represents an important opening towards growth and prosperity, but the poorest cities of the global South, notably in Africa, have struggled to attract outside investment beyond the primary commodity and minerals extraction sectors. All the same, many African cities, including Dakar, Accra, Lagos, Kigali, Nairobi, and, of course, Johannesburg, are increasingly participating in the modern world economy as entrepreneurial centres in their own right, and local economic development policies in many parts of the continent are seeking to strengthen the networks and productivity of the informal economy as well.

Box 3.1. The Shoe Industry of Marikina City, Philippines

Marikina City lies in the far northeast of the Manila Metropolitan Area. For over a century it has functioned as the principal centre of the Filipino shoe industry. Like much small-scale enterprise in both rich and poor countries, the industry is organized into a tight spatial cluster of firms (see Fig. 3.4) that often work together in various kinds of subcontract relations and that share a common labour market. Most of these firms are quite small and few of them employ more than ten workers. Wages are notably low in the Marikina shoe industry, and the main output consists of cheap shoes fabricated in both leather and synthetic materials for the domestic market. Almost all of the firms within the industry are family enterprises owned by individuals with roots that go deep into the local community. A distinctive intra-family division of labor is discernible in many shoe factories, where the wife is frequently engaged in financial and commercial tasks and the husband in shop-floor supervision. Some child labour is also to be found in the industry. Until the 1980s, the shoe industry in the Philippines was protected by high tariff barriers, but over the 1990s trade liberalization accelerated greatly. One effect of this shift has been a notable rise in imports of foreign shoes into the country with China leading the way as the main source of supply. This state of affairs has forced many Marikina shoe manufacturers to close down in recent years. One response to this state of affairs on the part of local manufacturers and policy makers has been to attempt to upgrade the quality of shoes produced so that they can fend off competition from imports and contest niches in international markets.

Fig. 3.5 Repair and recycling of old cooking oil cans, Mumbai, India. *Source* National Geographic, http://ngm.nationalgeographic.com/ngm/0705/feature3/gallery7.html. Published with permission of Magnum Photos

3.6   A Variegated and Uneven Mosaic

One way in which we can begin to make sense of some of the more recent trends and patterns described in this chapter is to put them in the context of the multi-dimensional global system of cities outlined in Chap. 1. A world-wide network or lattice of large cities and extended city-regions has emerged since the end of the 20th century, almost all of them characterized by dynamic economies, with multiple links and connections to each other as well as to many different small and medium-sized urban areas, agricultural zones and areas of resource extraction.

The core cities and city-regions that make up this worldwide lattice have populations in the multiple millions, and in some cases in the tens of millions (see Table 2.3), and are found in both the global North and the global South. These cities are the preeminent sites of the segmented occupational and economic systems described earlier, though each of them has its own specific character reflecting its peculiar forms of economic activity. Accordingly, these cities compete and collaborate with one another across the globe in relation to their complementarities and correspondences. Interspersed within this dominant pattern of global city-regions are large numbers of small and medium-sized cities with an enormous diversity of economic characteristics.

Certainly, modes and levels of economic development differ greatly from one another across this global-urban system so that the forms of labour, livelihood and employment characteristic of each individual city also vary widely. Moreover, work activities not only differ greatly from one city to another but are also highly variegated both functionally and spatially within each individual city. Much of this variegation is, of course, an expression of the intra-urban division of labour.

Cities, then, are dense clusters of inter-related processes of production, work, and life. This inter-relatedness is also one of the principal foundations of what, following the sociologist Emile Durkheim, we might refer to as the organic solidarity of urban society, that is, the tightly-wrought interdependencies that hold cities together as centres of shared social, economic and public life. Equally, though, urban communities in capitalism are dense sites of private property, competitive economic relationships and socially selective forms of appropriation so that urban existence is also subject to intense contestatory pressures. The following chapter elaborates on these themes of the private and the public in cities in relation to the challenge of creating and finding urban shelter.

Further Reading

J. V. Henderson and J. F. Thisse (eds.). 2004. *Handbook of Regional and Urban Economics.* Amsterdam: Elsevier.

Hutton, T. A. 2016. *Cities and the Cultural Economy.* Abingdon: Routledge

Macharia, K. 1997. *Social and Political Dynamics of the Informal Economy in African Cities,* Lanham, MD : University Press of America.

Peck, J. 1996. *Work-place : the Social Regulation of Labour Markets: Perspectives on economic change.* New York: Guilford Press.

Scott, A J, and G Garofoli, eds. 2007. *Development on the Ground: Clusters, Networks and Regions in Emerging Economies.* London: Routledge.

Storper, M, T Kemeny, N Makarem, and T Osman. 2015. *The Rise and Fall of Urban Economies: Lessons from San Francisco and Los Angeles.* Berkeley: University of California Press.

S. Yusuf and K. Nabeshima . 2010. *Changing the Industrial Geography in Asia: The Impact of China and India.* Washington, D.C.: World Bank Publications.

Additional data sources

For a general view of global urbanization processes: United Nations. 2009. *World Urbanization Prospects*. http://esa.un.org/unpd/wup/index.htm.

For demographic data on cities around the world: http://data.un.org/Data.aspx?d=POP&f=tableCode%3A240

For urban development indicators by country: http://data.worldbank.org/topic/urban-development

For business and economic conditions in leading world cities: http://www.mori-m-foundation.or.jp/english/ius2/gpci2/

For statistics and other information on the informal economy: http://wiego.org/wiego/core-programmes/statistics and http://laborsta.ilo.org/informal_economy_E.html

Chapter 4
Housing

4.1 The Challenge of Shelter

The expansion of urban economies has been accompanied by constant migration of people to cities in search of opportunities for work and livelihood, as discussed in the previous chapter. There are other reasons for living in cities such as seeking refuge from conflict, or being forced to move there when livelihoods elsewhere are threatened. Urban dwellers' children add to the numbers as well, so underlying high or low natural birth and death rates can set a baseline of rapid urban growth or generate a tendency for settlements to decline. As a result of all these processes, the number of people living in urban settlements expands and declines at different rates in different contexts (see Box 4.1).

Box 4.1 Querying the growth of urban populations

Thus far in this short book we have presented urban populations and the growth rates as known facts. In fact they are estimates whose veracity varies greatly by time and space. Severe problems with the poverty of data continue to the present in many of the poorest countries of the world.

The growth in urban populations, and of the number of people living in cities compared to other settlements, involves many different factors. In Africa, for example, urban birth rates generally remain high, adding more people to cities as they are born there, only slightly less than in rural areas, but as rural death rates are higher the proportion of population in cities is generally expanding. Nonetheless, there have been persistent overestimates of the rate of growth of cities in Africa, not helped by the fact that censuses have not been regularly conducted. In fact, at times, especially after the widespread economic crisis of the 1980s across the continent, there has been strong evidence of relative stagnation and even reversal in urban growth. Often cities seem to expand rapidly because growing numbers of people settling in nearby

---

© The Author(s) 2016
J. Robinson et al., *Working, Housing: Urbanizing*,
SpringerBriefs in Global Understanding, DOI 10.1007/978-3-319-45180-0_4

agricultural areas leads to these places being reclassified as urban. In India, in the decade to 2015 nearly 30 % of urban growth was a result of the reclassification of existing settlements and not rural to urban migration; and in China between 1990 and 2005 nearly 120 million people were added to cities in this way. Why do predictions about urban populations matter? Knowing where people are living informs decisions about where to invest resources for services, employment or humanitarian support.

No matter why people move to cities, finding secure shelter and the basic services to sustain life is often a significant challenge. The World Bank estimates that up to one billion people across the world live in shelter that is either of poor quality, lacks basic infrastructural services such as water or sewerage (thus making for unsafe living conditions) or is insecure in that the residents have no clear rights to their dwelling places (the controversial term "slum" is often used to describe these settlements—see Box 4.2). One of the major challenges for cities of the future, then, concerns not only how they can offer people opportunities to find decent work and wages, but also how urban populations will be housed.

Box 4.2 A note on the term "slum"

This term usually has derogatory connotations and can suggest that a settlement needs replacement or can legitimate the eviction of its residents. However, it is a difficult term to avoid for at least three reasons. First, some networks of neighbourhood organizations choose to identify themselves with a positive use of the term, partly to neutralize these negative connotations; one of the most successful is the National Slum Dwellers Federation in India. Second, the only global estimates for housing deficiencies, collected by the United Nations, are for what they term "slums". And third, in some nations, there are advantages for residents of informal settlements if their settlement is recognized officially as a "slum"; indeed, the residents may lobby to get their settlement classified as a "notified slum". Where the term is used [here], it refers to settlements characterized by at least some of the following features: a lack of formal recognition on the part of local government of the settlement and its residents; the absence of secure tenure for residents; inadequacies in provision for infrastructure and services; overcrowded and sub-standard dwellings; and location on land less than suitable for occupation. For a discussion of more precise ways to classify the range of housing submarkets through which those with limited incomes buy, rent or build accommodation, (text from D. Satterthwaite, 2016, "A New Urban Agenda?" *Environment and Urbanization*, 28, p. 3).

In the 1990s the goal of improving the quality of urban housing was adopted by the United Nations, and in the year 2000 their "Millennium Development Goals" set a target to achieve a significant improvement in the lives of 100 million "slum" dwellers by the year 2020. The 2015 UN report on these Development Goals noted that the overall proportion of the urban population living in "slums" in low and middle-income countries fell from approximately 39.4 % in 2000 to 29.7 % in 2014. But given the rapid processes of urbanization that persist in many parts of the world, the absolute numbers of people thought to be living in poor quality housing in cities actually increased to over 880 million urban residents compared to 792 million reported in 2000 and 689 million in 1990.[1] The growing significance of urban concentrations across the world has seen a renewed focus on improving the quality of life in cities, with a specific *Urban* Sustainable Development Goal (SDG) declared by the UN in September 2015, to "make cities and human settlements inclusive, safe, resilient and sustainable."

While every city has its own distinctive story of how housing has been developed and used, and of how people find their way to settle in different areas of the city, there has also been a lot of *sharing of ideas* around the world about how to meet the challenges of providing housing, especially through networks of cities and urban professionals, and through international organizations such as the World Bank and the United Nations. As a result there are often strong similarities in housing policies and design across different cities.

We can also detect some *overarching processes* which shape who lives where in cities. Above all, *markets* in land and housing help to sort the internal spaces of cities into different areas by income with affordability being a major limitation on where it is possible to find accommodation; *social divisions* like ethnicity, race, religion or political affiliation can also draw residents into or direct them away from certain neighbourhoods for safety or sociability reasons; and *powerful interests* or *violence* might leave people with little choice as to where they can find shelter. As it is such an important part of being able to survive in the city, housing is often the focus of *protests* and political demands. Sustaining life in cities rests, to a large extent, on securing rights to shelter and to the basic services often tied to houses, like water, energy, and waste removal. These *rights to the city* have been pressed on national governments in different countries by popular mobilization, resulting in state involvement in housing delivery in many cities, and they are also an important part of international development agendas. Access to housing not only supports important welfare goals such as improving health and widening access to services, but housing also provides opportunities for residents, especially women, to generate an income through informal economic activities or renting out rooms, and so it is also closely tied to economic development goals.

Nonetheless, the challenges of housing and basic services take on different forms in different cities. For some cities, there is simply not enough housing to cope with the growing urban population and many residents construct their own shelters in often very insecure situations. Where wages are low and livelihoods precarious, meeting housing needs can present an extreme challenge to households. In some cities, the intense development pressures due to globalization can make housing

---

[1] www.un.org/milleniumgoals/2015_MDG_Report.

unaffordable, so even if there is a large supply of accommodation many people on low or modest incomes often struggle to find somewhere to live, and vacant properties coexist with overcrowding and occupancy of apartments by multiple families or generations. This is exacerbated in cities that are strongly exposed to global property markets or to ambitious local redevelopment plans, and in highly unequal societies. One manifestation of this is "gentrification" involving the displacement of residents from low-income neighbourhoods in selected parts of the city, and their upgrading by means of vigorous property redevelopment, usually for the benefit of higher income groups.

To better understand the challenges of housing in cities we will look at a number of different urban contexts and, as with earlier chapters, we will trace some common historical trends explaining how cities have come to be the way they are today, and explore what processes will be shaping cities of the future.

4.2 Providing Housing Through States and Markets

4.2.1 Housing Needs and Housing as a Commodity

Numerous observers have written of the terrible conditions in which many people live and have lived in cities around the world. We noted above the writings of Friedrich Engels, an industrialist and collaborator of Karl Marx, who observed the brutal treatment of new industrial workers both in the workplace and in the shockingly overcrowded, damp and poorly constructed shelters in early industrial Manchester, England. As they grew rapidly across the world, cities in modern times drew philanthropists, housing reformers, city officials and a growing body of professionalized housing officers and planners as well as residents themselves to express concern and take various kinds of action against poor quality housing and its effects on people's health and the functioning of the city.

One of the perennial challenges has been how to provide adequate housing for those who live on meagre incomes. This brings to the fore some of the tensions of market economies, where housing and land are often seen as commodities whose function is to generate profit for land owners, developers, builders and landlords. The quality of housing therefore often depends on the nature of the economic opportunities available to residents, a factor that determines what they can afford. Housing quality also depends on whether states or other collective institutions play a role in facilitating access to housing. Historically in Europe, and in most countries today, renting housing from private landlords of various kinds has been the most prevalent mode of accessing accommodation, including in informal settlements. The evident tension between landlords' search for profit and the affordability of housing for the tenant, as well as the difficulties of ensuring good quality and sufficient quantity of housing through the market has led to various initiatives to shape housing on the part of the state.

4.2.2 State Interventions

Some of the earliest forms of "social" housing for the poor in Western cities were rental properties developed as philanthropic investments, where a guaranteed but low return to the investor was proposed, and where tenants received often quite intrusive supervision and support in organizing their finances and their lifestyles in the new homes. Many planned 19th century factory towns such as Saltaire in the UK and Pullman in the USA also displayed analogous forms of paternalism. But as housing issues came to the fore in local and national politics through the 20th century, states themselves became increasingly involved in regulating housing conditions through laws and standards.

Concerns grew about how to solve the health and social problems associated with poor housing, and a category of "slum" housing developed during the 19th century, defined by overcrowding, poverty, and the poor physical state of buildings. Such areas have often been targeted for demolition, and their populations removed to new housing—or simply displaced and left to find alternative places to live. More generally, areas which are home to poorer residents are vulnerable to removal if they are on land which powerful actors such as states, businesses and wealthy residents would like to see redeveloped, often leading to gentrification and displacement.

States also began taking responsibility for implementing ideas about what makes for a good city, notably how different activities and buildings should be arranged in the city. Urban planning addresses issues such as which land uses should be located close to one another, or should be kept apart through zoning rules. Urban spatial planning can be very helpful in cities, where so many often incompatible activities jostle for space, but it has also been used to place restrictions on where different groups can live or to remove people from areas that contravene the "plan." For example, housing for the poor can often be effectively excluded from wealthy areas of the city by zoning limitations on building multi-family properties; or the existence of formal Masterplans has been used in litigation by middle classes in some Indian cities, such as Delhi, to enforce the removal of longstanding informal settlements. The development of planning interventions which support and work with the aspirations of the poor and the solutions which they themselves devise is an urgent element of finding more effective and inclusive solutions to shelter needs in cities.

Planning visions of how neighbourhoods and cities should be organized and designed have influenced city development around the world. One prominent example of this is the idea of the "Garden City", initially associated with British urban planners, Ebenezer Howard and Patrick Geddes. This and allied ideas circulated widely, proposing that "new" cities or suburbs be built with houses arranged around communal facilities in healthy, greenfield sites with socially mixed populations and selected restrictions on socially undesirable activities (such as frequenting bars). Housing following these principles was developed through the middle decades of the 20th century in many cities around the world—from Tel

Fig. 4.1 Garden City—White City Tel Aviv (aerial view of dizengoff circus tel aviv, and surrounding district, 1951). http://gpophotoheb.gov.il/fotoweb

Aviv to Cape Town (see Fig. 4.1). These ideas also partly influenced the layout of segregated neighbourhoods built for African people in British colonial Africa, and in other cities such as Kinshasa. The principles of neighbourhood design in suburbs across the US, and, at a very different scale, the massive housing blocks or "mikrorayons" (microdistricts) built throughout the Soviet Union, all embody some principles drawn from the garden city idea, such as limiting the flow of vehicles on residential streets, and providing enclosed communal spaces within clusters of housing. These ideas continue to have relevance today, for example, inspiring a major new satellite city development, Lingang, on the outskirts of Shanghai.

While state involvement in housing provision first emerged in the 19th century, it was primarily after the Second World War that large-scale state intervention in housing became prominent. At this time, extensive developments appeared, such as working-class housing on the outskirts of Paris, council housing estates in the UK, public housing in a number of US cities, such as New York and Chicago, mass housing provision across the former Soviet Union and central Europe, and extensive but initially racially segregated provision of housing in many African and Asian cities (e.g. Johannesburg; Nairobi, Singapore, Mumbai). In these types of intervention, central state funding was mobilized directly to construct houses, or was used to subsidize private developers in various ways. The shift from private rental of accommodation to the state as the major landlord was significant in many cities. Access to housing was organized through state bureaucracies in both the West and the Soviet context, leading some commentators to point out a number of similarities in urban developments across these politically very different contexts at this time. In poorer country contexts, however, these kinds of housing developments were limited in scope, and were seldom able to develop financial models which allowed housing to reach beyond the middle classes (although apartheid South Africa was an important exception to this, delivering hundreds of thousands of homes to those African people permitted to live in cities under the notorious pass laws from the 1950s to the 1970s).

4.2.3   Private Finance

A separate strand of housing provision has been through private home ownership largely in suburban or peripheral locations. This is often associated with individual mortgages and financing through bank loans or more specialist building societies/home loan banks supporting individual home ownership. The latter developed in the late 19th century in the UK and USA pooling resources in a cooperative 'self-help' process but they transmuted into more conventional finance marketing in the 20th century. Where mortgage markets are weakly developed, individuals pay for housing purchases through individual savings or find other sources of financing, such as co-operative ventures, families or informal savings groups.

The growth of housing through private ownership is most characteristically associated with the expansion of the middle classes and the high wage/mass consumption growth path of the US under Fordism (as identified earlier). A coincidence of interests between the state, car industry and property developers led to the consolidation of suburbs as the norm for housing delivery. The result is often a sprawling multi-nodal city dependent on private cars and with very limited public transit infrastructure. This model has been important in cities in different parts of the world, for example in Southeast Asia since the 1980s where extended suburbanization, gated communities, satellite cities and freeway developments have led to a blurring of land use patterns in rural-urban fringe areas. These relatively haphazard and diverse extended peripheral developments constitute one of the predominant features of the contemporary city.

Where private home-ownership becomes the dominant mode of housing provision, this can create a significant problem of access to housing for the very poorest citizens for whom mortgage financing is usually not feasible. This was perhaps most vividly demonstrated in 2008, when loans had been inadvisedly extended to high-risk, low-income homeowners in the US, and hidden in complex secondary financial instruments, thereby helping to instigate a global economic crisis. In the absence of effective state intervention, other private solutions often emerge, more commonly associated with private renting. For example, low quality dense and relatively high-rise apartment blocks or "tenements" are common, with low-cost and frequently sub-divided apartments occupied by a number of families. Built (or converted to multi-family or residential use from existing buildings) by private individuals with little regulatory oversight, these predominate in some central city areas in South America as they do in many sprawling residential areas of African cities today and in "urban villages" in China where villages have been incorporated into expanding metropolitan regions providing villages with an opportunity to develop their land to meet burgeoning housing needs. Tenements were also historically important in 19th and early 20th century European cities.

In the mid-1970s, affordability issues for the lowest income households in poorer countries were recognized in the promotion by the UN of in situ upgrading and "site and service" schemes as the solution. Here a combination of self-help, legalized tenure, subsidies and supported access to mortgage financing provided serviced sites (with no house, or a very rudimentary structure) which could then be incrementally developed by residents. This made more inroads into addressing housing need. A number of problems emerged, however, including the capture of benefits by the middle classes, the high costs of land, and continuing affordability issues for the very poorest, which undermined the success of this policy initiative. In the end, where states and markets have failed, urban residents in many cities have occupied land and built their own shelter, often in very precarious situations.

4.3 Housing Solutions for the Future City

A range of models therefore exist around the world to inform choices about how states and communities might provide for housing needs in the future.

In contexts like Singapore and Hong Kong governments have played a continuing strong role in housing provision. In Singapore in 2009, 82 % of the population lived in housing governed and delivered by a public body, the Housing and Development Board (Fig. 4.2). But the intriguing aspect of this model is that 87 % of the population own their own homes (up from 9 % in 1960). Both Singapore and Hong Kong have developed a hybrid model in which individuals own apartments, but the state continues to own the land and to benefit financially over the long term from the increases in land value associated with housing, infrastructure and planning-related developments. Private developers lease land and gain profit from building and selling the apartment blocks, but the state retains the ability to benefit from the increased value of the land. They are also able to bid to direct new developments or oversee the redevelopment of existing properties.

This stands in strong contrast to the model of housing development in Chile, for example, (and copied in places like Mexico, Turkey and South Africa) where while states subsidize houses for the very poor, or provide support for low- to middle-income residents to purchase houses or apartments, they pass on the opportunity to earn profits from the land, housing and financing to individuals and private sector developers. Land costs and limited subsidies drive developers to seek cheap land, usually very inconveniently located in peripheral areas of the city. These challenges of the costs of land and poor location of housing have also beset the experience of mass housing delivery in Hong Kong, where large numbers of poor

Fig. 4.2 Housing development board properties in Singapore (Bukit Batok New Town, built c. 1985). *Source* http://www.teoalida.com/world/singapore/

residents and migrants placed greater strain on the housing delivery system. This reminds us that Singapore is perhaps unusual in having experienced rapid economic growth, and having been able to closely control population growth as a city-state. Nonetheless, the Singapore model in which land value increases are socialized and ownership is retained by the state might represent an interesting alternative way of meeting the housing challenges of both poorer and wealthier cities.

More generally, the Singapore example reminds us that housing developments are increasingly less easy to characterize as "state" or "market", and many actual cases entail a complex mix of state, markets and self-provisioning in providing shelter for urban dwellers. In reform-era China, public housing was sold cheaply to tenants, so that from a situation in 1981 where more than 80 % of the population lived in state owned housing, often located in close proximity to their workplace, by 2010 more than 80 % of the urban population owned their own homes. As house prices have risen dramatically in large cities, new migrants, poorer residents and young people who never benefited from the earlier sale of public housing find it increasingly difficult to find accommodation. Affordability issues undermined the capacity of this market-dominated housing strategy to provide for urban residents and by 2008 a state-led programme for delivering a mix of social, rental, affordable (subsidized) and market housing in mass housing developments was initiated.

Another solution to housing need comes from urban dwellers themselves, where they have self-organized to locate land, source materials and provide the labour to build their own shelter. This can be a precarious option, with people settling in areas of the city which might be subject to flooding or landslides, far from the centre of

Fig. 4.3 Ciudad Nezahualcóyotl in Mexico City. *Source* courtesy of Sonia Madrigal, http://soniamadrigal.com

town, or which residents don't have the legal right to occupy. However, land invasions, or occupations are sometimes well-organized affairs, and can involve powerful actors, such as politicians, political parties, or a range of collective, informal or illegal organizations. These different groups might be involved in finding land, arranging for plots to be made available, sometimes planning the spatial arrangements of houses and communal facilities, and taking payment for land transfers and rent. Large areas of cities have emerged through these processes, for example Ciudad Nezahualcóyotl in Mexico City, where over a million people now live, and where increasingly formal retail and industrial activities and even a university are being developed (Fig. 4.3).

In fact "informal" or popular housing is seldom disorganized, but usually involves a mix of both state and popular actors as well as legal and illegal actions. In South American cities, where state provision of housing has been minimal over many decades, securing services and entitlements to land have been a major focus of citizens' movements; and there is now a long tradition of slowly improving the quality of housing and services on peripheral land acquired relatively cheaply by poorer residents. Residents themselves incrementally extend their shelters and improve the quality of materials, and the state finally brings in services and transport connections, often after extensive political mobilization by residents. Medellin in Colombia, for example, has become very famous for the cable cars which have been developed to connect the central city areas to such informal areas or *barrios* which have been located in steep, poorly located areas of town (Fig. 4.4).

Fig. 4.4 Medellin cable cars. *Source* courtesy of Julio Davila, https://www.bartlett.ucl.ac.uk/dpu/metrocables/media-gallery

Government involvement in the expansion and consolidation of informal housing can be significant. In some situations, tacit or even quite explicit support from governments can see the large-scale development of informal housing as a way to solve problems of very rapid urbanization. In Istanbul, as new migrants from the countryside arrived through the 1980s, the Islamic parties in the city fostered informal settlements known as *gecekondus*, which both met housing needs and provided a base for building a political base amongst the more religious new immigrants. Perhaps the most famous example of this phenomenon is to be found in China, where "urban villages" have made a major contribution to housing the massive flows of new migrants to these cities (See Box 4.1 above). Former villagers now own and manage often very dense, high-rise housing developments in and close to major cities. While these have a de facto acceptance by the authorities, they are very vulnerable to redevelopment pressures from diverse state and municipal agencies. In Istanbul, too, the huge opportunities for profiting from alternative land uses for informal areas have more recently seen major urban renewal initiatives by the state, removing *gecekondu* residents (and increasingly residents of older, more run-down and lower rise areas of the city) to very distant new housing estates where, following the Chilean model, mortgages are made available to very poor households to acquire tiny apartments. These strategies have freed up large areas of land for controversial and profitable developments in central areas, which have been linked to corruption in the government. In theory this releases some profits for cross-subsidization of housing for the poor, but the housing remains largely unaffordable, and, being removed to the outskirts of the city, has had devastating consequences as people can no longer access employment opportunities; supportive family and neighbourhood relationships have also been severed.

A widely discussed policy idea suggests that residents in informal settlements should receive secure property rights. This would help them to feel confident about their future, encouraging investment and upgrading of structures, and see them able to use their investment in housing to support other goals, perhaps accessing financing to set up their own businesses. These ideas, made popular by Hernando de Soto from Peru in his book, *The Mystery of Capital*, have encountered some practical difficulties in places where state capacity is limited. It can be easier for better educated and wealthier people to organize to register their property rights, for example, and sometimes powerful agents might usurp the entitlements of the poor. Also this approach runs the risk of exposing poor people to subsequent pressures to sell their property for redevelopment. In Brazil, special legislation has been passed to protect poor communities by preventing the consolidation of small plots into larger holdings, which would make them attractive to developers and wealthier residents.

Policy ideas and practices in relation to informal housing have also emerged from the residents of these areas themselves. The important international movement originating in Mumbai, the Slum and Shack Dwellers International, has developed a programme of transnational exchange involving sharing their bottom-up model of self-enumeration and self-organization by slum residents to counter removal threats. The movement has spread to many cities across Asia and Africa (see Box 4.3). They also encourage residents to build their own plans for redevelopment and to work with authorities to create financial arrangements for housing developments which enable access to housing for the very poor. They have become involved in an initiative from the United Nations and the World Bank, the Cities Alliance, one of whose major ambitions is to see the elimination of "slums", and who encourage and support slum upgrading initiatives.

Box 4.3 Shack and Slum Dwellers International (SDI)

Background to the SDI: In 1974, shack dwellers in Mumbai who had resisted eviction from their neighbourhood through collecting information about themselves to negotiate more effectively with the authorities formed the basis for a National Slum Dwellers Federation of India. As some key figures in the movement note, explaining that there is only one toilet seat per 800 residents in the slum of Dharavi in Mumbai had a much stronger impact when negotiating with government than more general demands for rights. Very often governments have no records of informal settlements, and no idea how many people live there or the conditions of these areas. This initial group subsequently linked with pavement dwellers groups in the 1980s, and a growing number of women's savings groups, to form a wide network working with similar enumeration methods, the Indian Alliance. Building alliances at the city scale helped poor residents gain a stronger voice to develop and implement solutions. By the 1990s, this model expanded further as the groups began to hold international exchanges to share this model for developing the voice of the poor in urban planning. The Shack/Slum Dwellers International was formally set up by eight national federations in 1996, and many other federations have since joined. A strategic association with the Cities Alliance and the wider dissemination of the SDI method has seen a growing international use of this model of community self-enumeration and involvement in urban development.

For details see Sheela Patel, Carrie Baptist and Celine D'Cruz, 2012, "Knowledge is power—informal communities assert their right to the city through SDI and community-led enumerations" *Environment and Urbanization*, 24, 13–26).

Also there is a talk by Sheela Patel, one of the organizers of the SDI) at http://unhabitat.org/the-federation-model-of-community-organizing-sheela-patel-slum-dwellers-international/.

4.4   The Future Politics of Shelter

In many of the examples we have discussed here, from Singapore to Chile and Istanbul, it is clear that the ability to realize profits from developing urban land plays an increasingly important role in housing. On the one hand, in order to realize very large scale housing developments governments will usually rely on major developers. Issues concerning the impacts of land costs on profitability and affordability drive such developments to more distant locations and often the investments in infrastructure, transport and services necessary for ensuring inclusive participation in the city are not delivered. High transport costs and inconvenient location mean that even subsidized developments can end up benefitting the middle classes (who can afford the transport costs) rather than the poor (who can't afford to be so far from opportunities to make a living). More generally investment in urban property, often involving very large-scale developments in and around major cities, has come to be a significant contributor to economic growth and to the profitability of capitalist enterprises globally. In this context, meeting housing need competes with other profitable uses of land, and delivering housing for the poor often relies on generating profits from the sale and use of land—whether this is owned by the state (in China and Singapore, for example), or planned by the state for private sector speculation (as in Europe and the US).

Certainly, the sometimes inventive mix of agents and processes involved in delivering housing, including the impressive agency of urban dwellers themselves, holds out some promise in the search for shelter solutions for cities of the future. The potential to upgrade and improve well-located informally developed housing at a modest cost is recognized by many housing analysts as an essential part of meeting future housing needs. But it is also the case that the mix of state ambition and the search for profits by global investors presents some threats both to these settlements and to our collective urban futures.

A major danger is that many urban residents around the world face removal and upheaval from environments where closely interwoven opportunities for liveli-hoods, shelter and social relationships have been forged over many years. Whether this entails the displacement of residents from social housing in Europe, the redevelopment of slums in India, or the formal incorporation and redevelopment of Chinese urban villages, the future of the many hundreds of millions of urban dwellers for whom shelter is a daily challenge in terms of availability, affordability, and healthy living looks precarious and will be determined through various com-binations of ambitious state strategies, the widespread global shift of capital investment into urban property development, and the actions of often unpredictable institutions caught up in local power relationships.

This is as much a concern in the rapidly growing cities of middle-income countries as it is in economically prominent "global" cities like London. The scale, profitability and security of property investments in the wealthiest cities attracts the attention of global corporate capital and encourages ambitious infrastructure development by the state to support this. In London, for example, this means that poorer households, squeezed in terms of incomes by the changing form of work under corporate globalization, are being displaced from the central city and even relatively well-paid middle class residents are priced out of accommodation; widespread child poverty is being entrenched as a result of increasing housing costs and the loss of social housing to regeneration. In middle- and low-income cities ambitious developments, often on the outskirts of cities, can detract from the capacity to invest in the basic infrastructure provision desperately needed in existing parts of the city. Moreover, in stimulating further urban sprawl, environ-mentally unsustainable outcomes pose a threat to the future of the planet. Given the anticipated growth of the world's urban population over the next decades, with as many as 2.5 billion people predicted to be added to cities from 2010 to 2050, the future of providing shelter in cities presents one of the most significant challenges for humanity. This draws us then to the concluding chapter where we reflect more broadly on the future of urbanization.

Further Reading

Davis. M. 2006. *Planet of Slums*. London: Verso.

Haila, A. 2015. *Urban Land Rent: Singapore as a Property State*, Oxford: Wiley-Blackwell.

Hsing, Y-T. 2010. *The Great Urban Transformation: Politics of Land & Property in China*. New York: Oxford University Press.

Martine, G., McGranahan, G., Montgomery, M. and Fernández-Castilla, R. 2008. *The New Global Frontier: Urbanization, Poverty and Environment in the 21st Century*. London: Earthscan.

Mitlin, D. and Satterthwaite, D. 2013. *Urban Poverty in the Global South: Scale and Nature*. London: Routledge.

Parnell, S. and Oldfield, S. 2014. *The Routledge Handbook on Cities of the Global South*. London: Routledge.

Additional data sources

www.web.worldbank.org ("Urban Poverty and Slum Upgrading") brings together data and practical guidance on slum upgrading and addressing urban poverty from the World Bank and related organizations.

www.unhabitat.org has numerous resources and publications online to do with housing challenges and policy around the world

www.SDInet.org is the website of the Shack and Slum Dwellers International and has useful reports of the ways in which residents of informal areas have built capacity to engage with and shape development plans, as well as to oppose removal and displacement. Their publication, "Know your city, know your settlement", available on this website, provides an excellent introduction to their methodology and practices.

The website of the International Institute for Environment and Development has many useful and free publications reflecting its aim to link research and practice in collaborating with grassroots partners in urban areas around the world. http://www.iied.org/our-work

The Indian Institute for Human Settlements has numerous online publications and resources related to urbanization in India. http://iihs.co.in/knowledge-gateway/

Chapter 5
Urbanizing: The Future

In this short book we have presented an overview of some of the most urgent issues and questions facing city dwellers, planners and scholars about the development and social significance of cities. We have examined how cities first appeared and evolved through historical time; we have considered the basic logic of cities in terms of work and livelihood, employment and production; and we have looked intently at the phenomena of housing, shelter, and residential development and their effects on urban life. Clearly, from all that has gone before, cities are extraordinarily complex and problematical places that generate a continually shifting groundwork of predicaments and opportunities. What, we might ask, are the prospects for cities in the 21st century, and what future changes are likely to come into view?

The great urban utopian schemes that were proposed in the 19th and 20th centuries may seem to be a thing of the past. Numerous individuals, from Robert Owen in early 19th century Britain to Le Corbusier in mid-20th century France, set out plans for the reform of human society by means of ambitious projects intended to sweep away the debris of previous rounds of urbanization and to rebuild cities that they thought would put humanity on a new and higher plane of existence. While this kind of social utopianism is highly unfashionable today, perhaps because of its conspicuous failure ever to deliver on its various promises, ambitious plans for the reform of 21st century cities abound.

Some of these are developmental—like the Cities Alliance ambition for "cities without slums." In the light of what has been said in Chaps. 3 and 4 there are numerous unfinished tasks of economic development and social integration in contemporary cities, and these often vary widely depending on which parts of the world may be under consideration. It is in poorer countries, however, that these tasks are most urgently in need of attention. This is perhaps nowhere more the case than in many African countries where histories of colonial exploitation have combined with post-colonial political turmoil and often severe economic challenges to jeopardize their ability to cope with very high rates of urbanization. The developmental challenges of the urban future are significant—and have been recognized by the international agreement through the United Nations to set specific

© The Author(s) 2016
J. Robinson et al., *Working, Housing: Urbanizing*,
SpringerBriefs in Global Understanding, DOI 10.1007/978-3-319-45180-0_5

targets for Sustainable Urban Development to promote the rights of all urban dwellers to safe, inclusive and sustainable urban futures.

Many ambitious projects about urban futures are concerned with the environment. Although we have not explored this issue in this publication, cities all over the world today play a major role in engendering and exacerbating the contemporary environmental crisis. This role is manifest in the different ways in which they are sources of atmospheric, ground, and water pollution. The rising tide of urban population growth, increasing levels of disposable income, and uncontrolled sprawl mean that these problems are unlikely to disappear in the foreseeable future. Many commentators, though, are hopeful that the dynamism and innovative nature of urban centres might generate solutions. For example, increasing density of urban living potentially mitigates the environmental impact of a growing world population. Also, many municipalities, through networks and idea sharing with cities across the world, are making strenuous efforts to introduce effective environmental regulations. While cities are deeply implicated in processes of global warming, and the ever-increasing emission of carbon gases due to intensifying urban transport, economic activity, and domestic heating, lighting, and air-conditioning demands is having dramatically deleterious effects on the atmosphere, the potential to organize cities differently, with more public transport and green buildings, holds out hope for a better urban future.

The tension in this urban environmental agenda concerns the extent to which it might be co-opted by large corporations and wealthier urban residents to advance their own interests. The concept of eco-cities, for example, and wider ideas about sustainable or green urban design, have become part of the vigorous circulation of international planning norms around the globe by large western multinational architectural and engineering firms, as well as by successful Asian companies and state development agencies. As a result, it is not clear yet to what extent eco-cities will provide opportunities for socio-technical innovation in the search for more environmentally and socially inclusive forms of urban living, or whether they will form a basis for the further displacement and exclusion of the poor through so-called eco-friendly developments.

Ambitious plans for the future of cities also involve the intricate digital and infrastructural technologies that are now emerging under the banner of the "smart city", and which involve collecting and coordinating information, and building intelligent management systems. These technologies could also play a critical role in helping to address environmental concerns, especially given their enormous potential in regard to the coordination and delivery of public services, traffic control, and pollution monitoring. Under conditions of corporate globalization, the key question again is to what degree these technologies will be deployed in the pursuit of profit rather than meeting the demands of social equity. The question is especially urgent as much of the futuristic thinking here is bound up with the work of large corporations who spread these ideas through their marketing and sale of technology and the software they have developed. However, local political concerns can block and slow down the implementation of even very ambitious models—the Indian Government's goal to build 100 new smart cities to accommodate the anticipated urbanization of the next decades faces challenges not only of governance capacity, but also of locally based democratic opposition. The opportunities for digital networking amongst urban residents could support wider economic and social goals and might equally play a role in shaping future urban developments.

As the shifting character of globalization proceeds, an expanding worldwide network of major metropolitan areas or city-regions has made its decisive historical and geographical appearance. Representative examples are New York, Los Angeles, Paris, Amsterdam, Buenos Aires, São Paulo, Mexico City, Dakar, Johannesburg, Mumbai, Bangkok, Beijing, and Tokyo, but these are only a few of the literally hundreds of large city-regions that now exist throughout the modern world (see Table 2.3). City-regions constitute to an ever-increasing degree the basic engines of the global economy, for they generate collectively by far the dominant share of the economic output of modern capitalism. As such, they are converging in functional terms into an integrated planetary system as they become increasingly locked into mutual relationships of collaboration, trade, and population movement. The likelihood is that these city-regions will continue to grow in size and number, especially in much of the Global South.

Thus, China's urban population more than doubled over the period from 1990 to 2005, and is predicted to reach 1 billion soon after 2025. This has required the vast expansion of existing cities, and the emergence of new cities, such as Shenzhen, near Hong Kong. Shenzhen was a village of 10,000 in 1980 but is now one of the world's largest cities at over 10 million and is part of a much larger sprawling area of industry-led urbanization. Cities built as part of this vast urban expansion have become models for future urban development across Asia and elsewhere. The large finance, construction and development firms which build expertise in such developments find opportunities for similar large scale construction in many other cities, from Kigali (Rwanda) to Phnom Penh (Cambodia), eager to model themselves on the Asian success stories of Singapore, Seoul and Shanghai. Even in some of the poorest cities of the world, then, plans are underway to develop large-scale new satellite cities. At the right price housing in these developments is finding purchasers amongst the middle classes who seek better living conditions. An interesting art intervention (see Fig. 5.1) from the Kinshasa-based sculptor Bodys Isek Kingelez, reminds us that modernist dreams of replacing run-down and problem-ridden cities with a new, vertical, exciting urbanism can incite interest even as they might also constitute problematical fantasies which can easily lead to serious over-reach and socially regressive public spending.

Certainly, one of the deepest challenges of some of the more ambitious concepts about urban futures concerns who benefits from them. In particular, what aspects of city life are to be organized under the rules of private property and what aspects are to be elements of a more communal form of existence? A major question concerning both the present and the future revolves around the status of the city as a place of public benefits. In capitalism, with the privileged role that it ascribes to

Fig. 5.1 Bodys Isek Kingelez: "Project for Kinshasa for the Third Millenium, 1997." *Source* https://en.louisiana.dk/exhibition/africa

individual behavior, competition, and markets, the city has frequently been seen by both social scientists and ordinary citizens as essentially a site of anomie, detachment, individualism, and antagonism. This way of seeing things, however, overlooks one of the primary features of the urbanization process, namely, that it is a collective outcome that is very much greater than the sum of the parts. This state of affairs leads on to the further insight that huge swaths of urban life are dependent on what the Nobel prize winner Elinor Ostrom has called "common pool resources," that is, assets that are held either by all or by designated groups of people. In the city, these assets take on a multitude of forms, ranging from the agglomeration economies that are one of the foundations of urban growth, through the public goods and services that are essential for the smooth operation of the city and the pursuit of urban social life, to the cultural and intellectual assets that every city accumulates in its traditions and institutions. The advantages and disadvantages of cities for social and economic life are in large degree the result of these many different resources. In other words, we must add to the Durkheimian notion of organic solidarity that is built into the intra-urban division of labor, the forms of solidarity that also come from the shared economic, social, and cultural resources that make up the urban commons. This state of affairs gives new urgency and meaning to the old refrain that we all have a right to the city.

Over the next few decades the expected growth across the planet in numbers of urban dwellers (in cities of all sizes from large city-regions to small towns) will be of the order of about 80 million people a year. The United Nations predicts that nearly one billion new urban dwellers will be added in Africa from 2010 to 2050, and around 1.5 billion in Asia over the same time period. This continued growth will assuredly augment the range and intensity of urban problems in the future. While corporate globalization has certainly stamped its mark on cities across the world, and will no doubt continue to do so, we can also expect that residents in cities everywhere will seek to forge their own ways of living and reproducing themselves, their families and wider communities, which means, too, contesting the agendas of both global economic actors and ambitious or predatory states. In addition, urban futures will be partly shaped by the social networks which city dwellers everywhere forge, as well as by the formulation of imaginative future possibilities. The urban anthropologist Filip de Boeck writing of Kinshasa, one of the world's most informalized cities, quotes the local writer, Vincent Lombume Kalimasi, to the effect that despite all the challenges people who live there face "The city is a never-ending construction. The city can never remain a passive victim. The city is, on the contrary, a place of possibility, the place that enables you to do and to act."

All of this indicates that the most socially and politically viable kinds of urban outcomes typically reflect inclusive, collective planning and coordination, responsive to the solutions urban dwellers find for themselves, and not just arbitrary impositions by ambitious bureaucrats, or the products of profit-seeking developers. Collective action is an essential component of an urban order which meets the needs of all residents. It is essential for ensuring the availability and continuity of the public resources of the city as well as for resolving the many conflicts, breakdowns and failures that are also always an intrinsic element of urbanization processes. In the present deepening climate of neoliberalism, even currently existing collective arrangements of association, planning and coordination are politically under threat from those who consider that the market is the most effective way of preserving the urban commons and dealing with urban challenges. Even so, rebuilding capacities for collective and state action in some of the poorest cities is recognized internationally as a priority for the 21st century. We feel that the imperative of collective action in urban affairs is all the more important given the need to deal with the alarmingly deepening divide in incomes and life chances that is present in cities in all parts of the world. These remarks suggest that above and beyond the *right to the city* we must also take seriously the normative idea of *the right to make the city*.

Further Reading

Bulkeley, H. *Cities and Climate Change*. London: Routledge.
Indian Institute for Human Settlements, 2011. *India 2011: Evidence*. http://iihs.co.in/wp-content/
    uploads/2013/12/IUC-Book.pdf.
Parnell, S. and Pieterse, E. 2014. *Africa's Urban Revolution*. London: Zed Books.
Satterthwaite, D. and Mitlin, D. 2014. *Reducing Urban Poverty in the Global South*. London:
    Routledge.
Simone, A. 2011. *City Life from Jakarta to Dakar: Movements at the Crossroads*. New York;
    London: Routledge
UN Habitat. 2016. *World Cities Report 2016*. Nairobi: United Nations Human Settlements
    Programme. http://wcr.unhabitat.org/main-report/
Wu, F. 2015. *Planning for Growth: Urban and Regional Planning in China*. London: RTPI and
    Routledge.

Erratum to: Working, Housing: Urbanizing

Erratum to:
J. Robinson et al., *Working, Housing: Urbanizing*,
SpringerBriefs in Global Understanding,
DOI 10.1007/978-3-319-45180-0

In the original version of this chapter, there were some errors in the preface text to be rephrased. The frontmatter and the book have been updated with the change.

The updated original online version for this book frontmatter can be found at
DOI 10.1007/978-3-319-45180-0

J. Robinson (✉)
Department of Human Geography, University College London, London, UK
e-mail: jennifer.robinson@ucl.ac.uk

A.J. Scott
Department of Geography and Department of Public Policy, University of California,
Los Angeles, USA

P.J. Taylor
Northumbria University, Newcastle upon Tyne, UK

P.J. Taylor
Loughborough University, Loughborough, UK

© The Author(s) 2016   E1
J. Robinson et al., *Working, Housing: Urbanizing*,
SpringerBriefs in Global Understanding, DOI 10.1007/978-3-319-45180-0_6